Working Papers: Chapters 1-15

Financial and Managerial Accounting or Corporate Financial Accounting

THIRTEENTH EDITION

Carl S. Warren
Professor Emeritus of Accounting
University of Georgia, Athens

James M. Reeve
Professor Emeritus of Accounting
University of Tennessee, Knoxville

Jonathan E. Duchac
Professor of Accounting
Wake Forest University

CENGAGE Learning

Australia • Brazil • Japan • Korea • Mexico • Singapore • Spain • United Kingdom • United States

CENGAGE Learning

ISBN: 978-1-285-86958-2

Cengage Learning
20 Channel Center Street
Boston, MA 02210
USA

Cengage Learning is a leading provider of customized learning solutions with office locations around the globe, including Singapore, the United Kingdom, Australia, Mexico, Brazil, and Japan. Locate your local office at **www.cengage.com/global**.

Cengage Learning products are represented in Canada by Nelson Education, Ltd.

To learn more about Cengage Learning Solutions, visit **www.cengage.com**.

Purchase any of our products at your local college store or at our preferred online store **www.cengagebrain.com**.

Printed in the United States of America
3 4 5 6 7 22 21 20 19 18

CONTENTS

(The online appendix Working Papers are available at www.cengagebrain.com.)

PREFACE

The working papers include problem-specific forms for preparing solutions for Exercises, A&B Problems, the Continuing Problem, and the Comprehensive Problems from the textbook. These forms, with preprinted headings, provide a structure for the problems, which will help you get started and save you time.

Based on students' testimonials and instructors' feedback, the forms in the working papers have been streamlined to make them simpler to use and to better reflect the changing environment of business. For example, the vertical rules that separated digits of numbers entered into journals, ledgers, and statements have been removed, making it easier to write in numbers.

Note that when entering whole amounts into the forms, your instructor will direct you on whether to include a decimal point and zeroes (e.g., 100.00) or to omit those (e.g., 100).

EXERCISE 1-1

a. 1. ______ 6. ______ 11. ______
2. ______ 7. ______ 12. ______
3. ______ 8. ______ 13. ______
4. ______ 9. ______ 14. ______
5. ______ 10. ______ 15. ______

b. ______

EXERCISE 1-2

______

EXERCISE 1-3

a. 1. ______ 6. ______
2. ______ 7. ______
3. ______ 8. ______
4. ______ 9. ______
5. ______ 10. ______

b. ______

EXERCISE 1-4

______

EXERCISE 1-5

______

EXERCISE 1-6

	Assets	=	Liabilities	+	Stockholders' Equity
a.	________	=	$376,000	+	$895,000
b.	$1,375,000	=	________	+	$855,000
c.	$863,500	=	$211,000	+	________

EXERCISE 1-7

a. ______________________

b. ______________________

c. ______________________

d. ______________________

e. ______________________

EXERCISE 1-8

a. ______________________

b. ______________________

c. ______________________

d. ______________________

e. ______________________

f. ______________________

EXERCISE 1-9

a. ______________________

b. ______________________

c. ______________________

d. ______________________

e. ______________________

EXERCISE 1-10

a. (1) Assets: ______________________

(2) Liabilities: ______________________

(3) Stockholders' equity: ______________________

b. (1) Assets: ______________________

(2) Liabilities: ______________________

(3) Stockholders' equity: ______________________

EXERCISE 1-10, Concluded

c. ____

____

____

____

____

EXERCISE 1-11

1. Expenses: ______________________________
2. Issuing common stock in exchange for cash: ______________________________
3. Dividends: ______________________________
4. Revenues: ______________________________

EXERCISE 1-12

1. ____________________
2. ____________________
3. ____________________
4. ____________________
5. ____________________
6. ____________________
7. ____________________
8. ____________________
9. ____________________
10. ____________________

EXERCISE 1-13

a. (1) ______________________________

(2) ______________________________

(3) ______________________________

(4) ______________________________

(5) ______________________________

(6) ______________________________

(7) ______________________________

b. ______________________________

c. ______________________________

d. ______________________________

e. ______________________________

EXERCISE 1-14

EXERCISE 1-15

Jupiter:		
Mars:		
Saturn:		
Venus:		

EXERCISE 1-16

1. Accounts Receivable: ______________________
2. Cash: ______________________
3. Common Stock: ______________________
4. Fees Earned: ______________________
5. Land: ______________________
6. Supplies: ______________________
7. Supplies Expense: ______________________
8. Utilities Expense: ______________________
9. Wages Expense: ______________________
10. Wages Payable: ______________________

EXERCISE 1-17

1. Accounts Receivable: ______________________
2. Cash: ______________________
3. Common Stock: ______________________
4. Fees Earned: ______________________
5. Land: ______________________
6. Supplies: ______________________
7. Supplies Expense: ______________________
8. Utilities Expense: ______________________
9. Wages Expense: ______________________
10. Wages Payable: ______________________

EXERCISE 1-18

a.

Retained Earnings Statement

EXERCISE 1-18, Concluded

b. ______________________

EXERCISE 1-19

Income Statement

Name ______________________________

EXERCISE 1-20

Freeman:

Heyward:

Jones:

Ramirez:

EXERCISE 1-21

a.

Balance Sheet

Balance Sheet

b.

EXERCISE 1-21, Concluded

c.

EXERCISE 1-22

a. 1. Accounts payable: ______
2. Cash equivalents: ______
3. Crude oil inventory: ______
4. Equipment: ______
5. Exploration expenses: ______
6. Income taxes payable: ______
7. Investments: ______
8. Long-term debt: ______
9. Marketable securities: ______
10. Notes and loans payable: ______
11. Notes receivable: ______
12. Operating expenses: ______
13. Prepaid taxes: ______
14. Sales: ______
15. Selling expenses: ______

b. ______

c. ______

EXERCISE 1-23

1. Cash received from fees earned: ______________________
2. Cash paid for expenses: ______________________
3. Cash paid for land: ______________________
4. Cash paid to owner for dividends: ______________________

EXERCISE 1-24

Statement of Cash Flows

EXERCISE 1-25

EXERCISE 1-25, Continued

(Optional)

Income Statement

Retained Earnings Statement

EXERCISE 1-25, Concluded

(Optional)

Balance Sheet

EXERCISE 1-26

a.

b.

c.

EXERCISE 1-27

a.

b.

c.

d.

PROBLEM 1-1 ___

1.

	Assets			= Liabilities +	Stockholders' Equity								
	Cash +	Accounts Receivable +	Supplies =	Accounts Payable +	Common Stock –	Dividends +	Fees Earned –	Rent Expense –	Salaries Expense –	Supplies Expense –	Auto Expense –	Misc. Expense
a.												
b.												
Bal.												
c.												
Bal.												
d.												
Bal.												
e.												
Bal.												
f.												
Bal.												
g.												
Bal.												
h.												
Bal.												
i.												
Bal.												
j.												
Bal.												

PROBLEM 1-1 ___, Concluded

2. ____

____

____

____

3. ____

____

4. ____

____

____

____

PROBLEM 1-2 ___

1.

Income Statement

2.

Retained Earnings Statement

PROBLEM 1-2 ___, Concluded

3.

Balance Sheet

4. ____

____

PROBLEM 1-3 ___

1.

Income Statement

2.

Retained Earnings Statement

PROBLEM 1-3 ___, Concluded

3.

Balance Sheet

4. (Optional)

Statement of Cash Flows

PROBLEM 1-4 ___

1.

	Assets		= Liabilities +	Stockholders' Equity								
	Cash +	Supplies =	Accounts Payable +	Common Stock –	Dividends +	Sales Comm. –	Rent Expense –	Salaries Expense –	Auto Expense –	Supplies Expense –	Misc. Expense
a.											
b.											
Bal.											
c.											
Bal.											
d.											
Bal.											
e.											
Bal.											
f.											
Bal.											
g.											
Bal.											
h.											
Bal.											
i.											
Bal.											

PROBLEM 1-4 ___, Continued

2.

Income Statement

Retained Earnings Statement

PROBLEM 1-4 ___, Concluded

Balance Sheet

This Page Not Used.

PROBLEM 1-5 ___

1.

ASSETS							=	LIABILITIES	+	STOCKHOLDERS' EQUITY		
Cash	+	Accounts Receivable	+	Supplies	+	Land	=	Accounts Payable	+	Common Stock	+	Retained Earnings
______	+	______	+	______	+	______	=	______	+	______	+	Retained Earnings
______							=	______	+	Retained Earnings		
______							=	Retained Earnings				

PROBLEM 1-5 ___, Continued

2.

	Assets				= Liabilities +	Stockholders' Equity										
	Cash +	Accts. Rec. +	Supplies +	Land =	Accounts Payable +	Common Stock +	Retained Earnings –	Dividends +	Dry Cleaning Revenue –	Dry Cleaning Exp. –	Wages Exp. –	Rent Exp. –	Supp. Exp. –	Truck Exp. –	Util. Exp. –	Misc. Exp.
Bal.																
a.																
Bal.																
b.																
Bal.																
c.																
Bal.																
d.																
Bal.																
e.																
Bal.																
f.																
Bal.																
g.																
Bal.																
h.																
Bal.																
i.																
Bal.																
j.																
Bal.																
k.																
Bal.																
l.																
Bal.																

PROBLEM 1-5 ___, Continued

3.

Income Statement

Retained Earnings Statement

PROBLEM 1-5 ___, Continued

Balance Sheet

4. (Optional)

Statement of Cash Flows

Name ______________________________

PROBLEM 1-6 ___

a. ______________________________

____

b. ______________________________

____

c. ______________________________

____

d. ______________________________

____

e. ______________________________

____

f. ______________________________

____

g. ______________________________

____

h. ______________________________

____

i. ______________________________

____

j. ______________________________

____

k. ______________________________

____

l. ______________________________

____

m. ______________________________

____

n. ______________________________

____

o. ______________________________

____

p. ______________________________

____

q. ______________________________

____

This Page Not Used.

CONTINUING PROBLEM

1.

	Assets			= Liabilities +	Stockholders' Equity											
	Cash +	Accts. Rec. +	Supplies =	Accounts Payable +	Common Stock –	Dividends +	Fees Earned –	Music Exp. –	Office Rent Exp. –	Equip. Rent Exp. –	Adv. Exp. –	Wages Exp. –	Util. Exp. –	Sup. Exp. –	Misc. Exp.
6/1															
6/2															
Bal.															
6/2															
Bal.															
6/4															
Bal.															
6/6															
Bal.															
6/8															
Bal.															
6/12															
Bal.															
6/13															
Bal.															
6/16															
Bal.															
6/22															
Bal.															
6/25															
Bal.															

CONTINUING PROBLEM, Continued

	Assets			= Liabilities +	Stockholders' Equity												
	Cash	+ Accts. Rec.	+ Supplies	= Accounts Payable	+ Common Stock	– Dividends	+ Fees Earned	– Music Exp.	– Office Rent Exp.	– Equip. Rent Exp.	– Adv. Exp.	– Wages Exp.	– Util. Exp.	– Sup. Exp.	– Misc. Exp.
6/29															
Bal.															
6/30															
Bal.															
6/30															
Bal.															
6/30															
Bal.															
6/30															
Bal.															
6/30															
Bal.															
6/30															
Bal.															
6/30															
Bal.															

CONTINUING PROBLEM, Continued

2.

Income Statement

3.

Retained Earnings Statement

CONTINUING PROBLEM, Concluded

4.

Balance Sheet

EXERCISE 2-1

Accounts Payable: ______________________

Advanced Payments for Equipment: ______________________

Air Traffic Liability: ______________________

Aircraft Fuel (Expense): ______________________

Aircraft Maintenance (Expense): ______________________

Aircraft Rent (Expense): ______________________

Cargo Revenue: ______________________

Cash: ______________________

Contract Carrier Arrangements (Expense): ______________________

Flight Equipment: ______________________

Frequent Flyer (Obligations): ______________________

Fuel Inventory: ______________________

Landing Fees (Expense): ______________________

Parts and Supplies Inventories: ______________________

Passenger Commissions (Expense): ______________________

Passenger Revenue: ______________________

Prepaid Expenses: ______________________

Taxes Payable: ______________________

EXERCISE 2-2

Account	Account Number
Accounts Payable.................	______
Accounts Receivable............	______
Cash	______
Common Stock.....................	______
Dividends.............................	______
Fees Earned.........................	______
Land	______
Miscellaneous Expense	______
Retained Earnings................	______
Supplies Expense	______
Wages Expense	______

EXERCISE 2-3

Balance Sheet Accounts

Acct. #	Account Name
	1. Assets
	2. Liabilities
	3. Stockholders' Equity

Income Statement Accounts

Acct. #	Account Name
	4. Revenue
	5. Expenses

EXERCISE 2-4

	Increase	Decrease	Normal Balance
Balance sheet accounts:			
Asset	(a) ___	(b) ___	Debit
Liability	(c) ___	Debit	(d) ___
Stockholders' Equity:			
Common Stock	Credit	(e) ___	(f) ___
Retained Earnings	(g) ___	(h) ___	Credit
Dividends	Debit	Credit	(i) ___
Income statement accounts:			
Revenue	(j) ___	(k) ___	Credit
Expense	(l) ___	Credit	Debit

EXERCISE 2-5

1. Accounts Payable: ______________________________
2. Accounts Receivable: ______________________________
3. Cash: ______________________________
4. Fees Earned: ______________________________
5. Insurance Expense: ______________________________
6. Dividends: ______________________________
7. Utilities Expense: ______________________________

EXERCISE 2-6

a. Accounts Payable: ______________________________
b. Accounts Receivable: ______________________________
c. Cash: ______________________________
d. Common Stock: ______________________________
e. Dividends: ______________________________
f. Fees Earned: ______________________________
g. Office Equipment: ______________________________
h. Rent Expense: ______________________________
i. Supplies: ______________________________
j. Wages Expense: ______________________________

EXERCISE 2-7

JOURNAL

PAGE

	DATE		DESCRIPTION	POST. REF.	DEBIT	CREDIT	
1							1
2							2
3							3
4							4
5							5
6							6
7							7
8							8
9							9
10							10
11							11
12							12
13							13
14							14
15							15
16							16
17							17
18							18
19							19
20							20
21							21
22							22
23							23
24							24
25							25
26							26
27							27
28							28
29							29
30							30
31							31
32							32
33							33
34							34
35							35
36							36

EXERCISE 2-8

a.

JOURNAL

PAGE 33

	DATE		DESCRIPTION	POST. REF.	DEBIT	CREDIT	
1							1
2							2
3							3
4							4
5							5

b., c., and d.

ACCOUNT ACCOUNT NO.

DATE		ITEM	POST. REF.	DEBIT	CREDIT	BALANCE DEBIT	BALANCE CREDIT

ACCOUNT ACCOUNT NO.

DATE		ITEM	POST. REF.	DEBIT	CREDIT	BALANCE DEBIT	BALANCE CREDIT

e. ____

EXERCISE 2-9

a.

JOURNAL PAGE

	DATE		DESCRIPTION	POST. REF.	DEBIT	CREDIT	
1							1
2							2
3							3
4							4
5							5
6							6
7							7
8							8
9							9
10							10
11							11
12							12

b.

Cash

Accounts Payable

Supplies

Fees Earned

Accounts Receivable

c.

EXERCISE 2-10

a.

b.

EXERCISE 2-11

a.

Accounts Payable

b.

Accounts Receivable

EXERCISE 2-11, Concluded

c.

Cash

EXERCISE 2-12

a.

b.

EXERCISE 2-13

a. and b.

	Account Debited		Account Credited	
Transaction	**Type**	**Effect**	**Type**	**Effect**
(1)	asset	+	stockholders' equity	+
(2)				
(3)				
(4)				
(5)				
(6)				
(7)				
(8)				
(9)				

EXERCISE 2-14

JOURNAL

PAGE

	DATE		DESCRIPTION	POST. REF.	DEBIT	CREDIT	
1							1
2							2
3							3
4							4
5							5
6							6
7							7
8							8
9							9
10							10
11							11
12							12
13							13
14							14
15							15
16							16
17							17
18							18
19							19
20							20
21							21
22							22
23							23
24							24
25							25
26							26
27							27
28							28
29							29
30							30
31							31
32							32
33							33
34							34
35							35
36							36

EXERCISE 2-15

a.

Unadjusted Trial Balance

b. ____

EXERCISE 2-16

Unadjusted Trial Balance

EXERCISE 2-17

EXERCISE 2-18

Unadjusted Trial Balance

EXERCISE 2-19

Error	(a) Out of Balance	(b) Difference	(c) Larger Total
1.	yes	$6,000	debit
2.			
3.			
4.			
5.			
6.			
7.			

EXERCISE 2-20

(Optional)

Unadjusted Trial Balance

EXERCISE 2-21

JOURNAL

PAGE

	DATE		DESCRIPTION	POST. REF.	DEBIT	CREDIT	
1							1
2							2
3							3
4							4
5							5
6							6
7							7
8							8
9							9

EXERCISE 2-22

JOURNAL

PAGE

	DATE		DESCRIPTION	POST. REF.	DEBIT	CREDIT	
1							1
2							2
3							3
4							4
5							5
6							6
7							7
8							8
9							9
10							10

EXERCISE 2-23

a. 1. Revenue: ______________________

____

2. Operating expenses: ______________________

____

3. Operating income: ______________________

____

b. ______________________

____

____

____

EXERCISE 2-24

a. **1.** Revenue: ____________________

2. Operating expenses: ____________________

3. Operating income: ____________________

b. ____________________

c. ____________________

PROBLEM 2-1 ___

1. and 2.

Cash

Accounts Receivable

Supplies

Prepaid Insurance

Automobiles

PROBLEM 2-1 ___, Continued

Equipment

Notes Payable

Accounts Payable

Common Stock

Professional Fees

Rent Expense

PROBLEM 2-1 ___, Continued

Salary Expense

Blueprint Expense

Automobile Expense

Miscellaneous Expense

PROBLEM 2-1 ___, Concluded

3.

Unadjusted Trial Balance

4. ____

PROBLEM 2-2 ___

1.

JOURNAL

PAGE

	DATE		DESCRIPTION	POST. REF.	DEBIT	CREDIT	
1							1
2							2
3							3
4							4
5							5
6							6
7							7
8							8
9							9
10							10
11							11
12							12
13							13
14							14
15							15
16							16
17							17
18							18
19							19
20							20
21							21
22							22
23							23
24							24
25							25
26							26
27							27
28							28
29							29
30							30
31							31
32							32
33							33
34							34
35							35

PROBLEM 2-2 ___, Continued

2.

Cash

Supplies

Accounts Payable

Common Stock

Dividends

Sales Commissions

PROBLEM 2-2 ___, Continued

Rent Expense

Office Salaries Expense

Automobile Expense

Supplies Expense

Miscellaneous Expense

PROBLEM 2-2 ___, Concluded

3.

Unadjusted Trial Balance

4. a. ______________________________

b. ______________________________

c. ______________________________

5. ______________________________

____

PROBLEM 2-3 ___

1.

JOURNAL

PAGE *1*

DATE		DESCRIPTION	POST. REF.	DEBIT	CREDIT

PROBLEM 2-3 ___, Continued

JOURNAL

PAGE 2

	DATE		DESCRIPTION	POST. REF.	DEBIT	CREDIT	
1							1
2							2
3							3
4							4
5							5
6							6
7							7
8							8
9							9
10							10
11							11
12							12
13							13
14							14
15							15
16							16
17							17
18							18
19							19
20							20
21							21
22							22
23							23
24							24
25							25
26							26
27							27
28							28
29							29
30							30
31							31
32							32
33							33
34							34
35							35
36							36

PROBLEM 2-3 ___, Continued

2.

GENERAL LEDGER

ACCOUNT *Cash* ACCOUNT NO. *11*

DATE		ITEM	POST. REF.	DEBIT	CREDIT	BALANCE DEBIT	BALANCE CREDIT

ACCOUNT *Accounts Receivable* ACCOUNT NO. *12*

DATE		ITEM	POST. REF.	DEBIT	CREDIT	BALANCE DEBIT	BALANCE CREDIT

ACCOUNT *Supplies* ACCOUNT NO. *13*

DATE		ITEM	POST. REF.	DEBIT	CREDIT	BALANCE DEBIT	BALANCE CREDIT

ACCOUNT *Prepaid Insurance* ACCOUNT NO. *14*

DATE		ITEM	POST. REF.	DEBIT	CREDIT	BALANCE DEBIT	BALANCE CREDIT

PROBLEM 2-3 ___, Continued

ACCOUNT *Equipment* ACCOUNT NO. *16*

DATE		ITEM	POST. REF.	DEBIT	CREDIT	BALANCE	
						DEBIT	CREDIT

ACCOUNT *Truck* ACCOUNT NO. *18*

DATE		ITEM	POST. REF.	DEBIT	CREDIT	BALANCE	
						DEBIT	CREDIT

ACCOUNT *Notes Payable* ACCOUNT NO. *21*

DATE		ITEM	POST. REF.	DEBIT	CREDIT	BALANCE	
						DEBIT	CREDIT

ACCOUNT *Accounts Payable* ACCOUNT NO. *22*

DATE		ITEM	POST. REF.	DEBIT	CREDIT	BALANCE	
						DEBIT	CREDIT

ACCOUNT *Common Stock* ACCOUNT NO. *31*

DATE		ITEM	POST. REF.	DEBIT	CREDIT	BALANCE	
						DEBIT	CREDIT

PROBLEM 2-3 ___, Continued

ACCOUNT *Dividends* ACCOUNT NO. *33*

DATE		ITEM	POST. REF.	DEBIT	CREDIT	BALANCE DEBIT	BALANCE CREDIT

ACCOUNT *Fees Earned* ACCOUNT NO. *41*

DATE		ITEM	POST. REF.	DEBIT	CREDIT	BALANCE DEBIT	BALANCE CREDIT

ACCOUNT *Wages Expense* ACCOUNT NO. *51*

DATE		ITEM	POST. REF.	DEBIT	CREDIT	BALANCE DEBIT	BALANCE CREDIT

ACCOUNT *Rent Expense* ACCOUNT NO. *53*

DATE		ITEM	POST. REF.	DEBIT	CREDIT	BALANCE DEBIT	BALANCE CREDIT

ACCOUNT *Utilities Expense* ACCOUNT NO. *54*

DATE		ITEM	POST. REF.	DEBIT	CREDIT	BALANCE DEBIT	BALANCE CREDIT

PROBLEM 2-3 ___, Continued

ACCOUNT *Truck Expense* ACCOUNT NO. *55*

DATE		ITEM	POST. REF.	DEBIT	CREDIT	BALANCE DEBIT	BALANCE CREDIT

ACCOUNT *Miscellaneous Expense* ACCOUNT NO. *59*

DATE		ITEM	POST. REF.	DEBIT	CREDIT	BALANCE DEBIT	BALANCE CREDIT

PROBLEM 2-3 ___, Concluded

3.

Unadjusted Trial Balance

4.

5.

This Page Not Used.

Name ______________________________

PROBLEM 2-4 ___

2. and 3.

JOURNAL

PAGE *18*

DATE		DESCRIPTION	POST. REF.	DEBIT	CREDIT

PROBLEM 2-4 ___, Continued

JOURNAL

PAGE *19*

	DATE		DESCRIPTION	POST. REF.	DEBIT	CREDIT	
1							1
2							2
3							3
4							4
5							5
6							6
7							7
8							8
9							9
10							10
11							11
12							12
13							13
14							14
15							15
16							16
17							17
18							18
19							19
20							20
21							21
22							22
23							23
24							24
25							25
26							26
27							27
28							28
29							29
30							30
31							31
32							32
33							33
34							34
35							35
36							36

PROBLEM 2-4 ___, Continued

1. and 3.

GENERAL LEDGER

ACCOUNT *Cash* ACCOUNT NO. *11*

DATE		ITEM	POST. REF.	DEBIT	CREDIT	BALANCE DEBIT	BALANCE CREDIT

ACCOUNT *Accounts Receivable* ACCOUNT NO. *12*

DATE		ITEM	POST. REF.	DEBIT	CREDIT	BALANCE DEBIT	BALANCE CREDIT

ACCOUNT *Prepaid Insurance* ACCOUNT NO. *13*

DATE		ITEM	POST. REF.	DEBIT	CREDIT	BALANCE DEBIT	BALANCE CREDIT

PROBLEM 2-4 ___, Continued

ACCOUNT *Office Supplies* ACCOUNT NO. *14*

DATE		ITEM	POST. REF.	DEBIT	CREDIT	BALANCE DEBIT	BALANCE CREDIT

ACCOUNT *Land* ACCOUNT NO. *16*

DATE		ITEM	POST. REF.	DEBIT	CREDIT	BALANCE DEBIT	BALANCE CREDIT

ACCOUNT *Accounts Payable* ACCOUNT NO. *21*

DATE		ITEM	POST. REF.	DEBIT	CREDIT	BALANCE DEBIT	BALANCE CREDIT

ACCOUNT *Unearned Rent* ACCOUNT NO. *22*

DATE		ITEM	POST. REF.	DEBIT	CREDIT	BALANCE DEBIT	BALANCE CREDIT

ACCOUNT *Notes Payable* ACCOUNT NO. *23*

DATE		ITEM	POST. REF.	DEBIT	CREDIT	BALANCE DEBIT	BALANCE CREDIT

PROBLEM 2-4 ___, Continued

ACCOUNT *Common Stock* ACCOUNT NO. *31*

DATE		ITEM	POST. REF.	DEBIT	CREDIT	BALANCE DEBIT	BALANCE CREDIT

ACCOUNT *Retained Earnings* ACCOUNT NO. *32*

DATE		ITEM	POST. REF.	DEBIT	CREDIT	BALANCE DEBIT	BALANCE CREDIT

ACCOUNT *Dividends* ACCOUNT NO. *33*

DATE		ITEM	POST. REF.	DEBIT	CREDIT	BALANCE DEBIT	BALANCE CREDIT

ACCOUNT *Fees Earned* ACCOUNT NO. *41*

DATE		ITEM	POST. REF.	DEBIT	CREDIT	BALANCE DEBIT	BALANCE CREDIT

ACCOUNT *Salary and Commission Expense* ACCOUNT NO. *51*

DATE		ITEM	POST. REF.	DEBIT	CREDIT	BALANCE DEBIT	BALANCE CREDIT

PROBLEM 2-4 ___, Continued

ACCOUNT *Rent Expense* ACCOUNT NO. *52*

DATE		ITEM	POST. REF.	DEBIT	CREDIT	BALANCE DEBIT	BALANCE CREDIT

ACCOUNT *Advertising Expense* ACCOUNT NO. *53*

DATE		ITEM	POST. REF.	DEBIT	CREDIT	BALANCE DEBIT	BALANCE CREDIT

ACCOUNT *Automobile Expense* ACCOUNT NO. *54*

DATE		ITEM	POST. REF.	DEBIT	CREDIT	BALANCE DEBIT	BALANCE CREDIT

ACCOUNT *Miscellaneous Expense* ACCOUNT NO. *59*

DATE		ITEM	POST. REF.	DEBIT	CREDIT	BALANCE DEBIT	BALANCE CREDIT

PROBLEM 2-4 ___, Concluded

4.

Unadjusted Trial Balance

5. a. ______________________

____

b.

JOURNAL PAGE

	DATE		DESCRIPTION	POST. REF.	DEBIT	CREDIT	
1							1
2							2
3							3
4							4

c. ______________________

This Page Not Used.

PROBLEM 2-5 ___

1.

Corrected Unadjusted Trial Balance

	DEBIT BALANCES	CREDIT BALANCES
Cash		
Accounts Receivable		
Supplies		
Prepaid Insurance		
Equipment		
Notes Payable		
Accounts Payable		
Common Stock		
Retained Earnings		
Dividends		
Fees Earned		
Wages Expense		
Rent Expense		
Advertising Expense		
Gas, Electricity, and Water Expense		
Miscellaneous Expense		

2. ______________________________

This Page Not Used.

CONTINUING PROBLEM

2. and 3.

JOURNAL

PAGE 1

	DATE		DESCRIPTION	POST. REF.	DEBIT	CREDIT	
1							1
2							2
3							3
4							4
5							5
6							6
7							7
8							8
9							9
10							10
11							11
12							12
13							13
14							14
15							15
16							16
17							17
18							18
19							19
20							20
21							21
22							22
23							23
24							24
25							25
26							26
27							27
28							28
29							29
30							30
31							31
32							32
33							33
34							34
35							35

CONTINUING PROBLEM, Continued

JOURNAL

PAGE 2

	DATE	DESCRIPTION	POST. REF.	DEBIT	CREDIT	
1						1
2						2
3						3
4						4
5						5
6						6
7						7
8						8
9						9
10						10
11						11
12						12
13						13
14						14
15						15
16						16
17						17
18						18
19						19
20						20
21						21
22						22
23						23
24						24
25						25
26						26
27						27
28						28
29						29
30						30
31						31
32						32
33						33
34						34
35						35
36						36

CONTINUING PROBLEM, Continued

JOURNAL

PAGE 3

	DATE		DESCRIPTION	POST. REF.	DEBIT	CREDIT	
1							1
2							2
3							3
4							4
5							5
6							6
7							7
8							8
9							9
10							10
11							11
12							12
13							13
14							14
15							15
16							16
17							17
18							18
19							19
20							20
21							21
22							22
23							23
24							24
25							25
26							26
27							27
28							28
29							29
30							30
31							31
32							32
33							33
34							34
35							35
36							36

CONTINUING PROBLEM, Continued

1. and 3.

GENERAL LEDGER

ACCOUNT *Cash* ACCOUNT NO. *11*

DATE		ITEM	POST. REF.	DEBIT	CREDIT	BALANCE	
						DEBIT	CREDIT

CONTINUING PROBLEM, Continued

ACCOUNT *Accounts Receivable* ACCOUNT NO. *12*

DATE	ITEM	POST. REF.	DEBIT	CREDIT	BALANCE	
					DEBIT	CREDIT

ACCOUNT *Supplies* ACCOUNT NO. *14*

DATE	ITEM	POST. REF.	DEBIT	CREDIT	BALANCE	
					DEBIT	CREDIT

ACCOUNT *Prepaid Insurance* ACCOUNT NO. *15*

DATE	ITEM	POST. REF.	DEBIT	CREDIT	BALANCE	
					DEBIT	CREDIT

ACCOUNT *Office Equipment* ACCOUNT NO. *17*

DATE	ITEM	POST. REF.	DEBIT	CREDIT	BALANCE	
					DEBIT	CREDIT

CONTINUING PROBLEM, Continued

ACCOUNT *Accumulated Depreciation—Office Equipment* ACCOUNT NO. *18*

DATE		ITEM	POST. REF.	DEBIT	CREDIT	BALANCE	
						DEBIT	CREDIT

(This account is not used in Chapter 2.)

ACCOUNT *Accounts Payable* ACCOUNT NO. *21*

DATE		ITEM	POST. REF.	DEBIT	CREDIT	BALANCE	
						DEBIT	CREDIT

ACCOUNT *Wages Payable* ACCOUNT NO. *22*

DATE		ITEM	POST. REF.	DEBIT	CREDIT	BALANCE	
						DEBIT	CREDIT

(This account is not used in Chapter 2.)

ACCOUNT *Unearned Revenue* ACCOUNT NO. *23*

DATE		ITEM	POST. REF.	DEBIT	CREDIT	BALANCE	
						DEBIT	CREDIT

CONTINUING PROBLEM, Continued

ACCOUNT *Common Stock* ACCOUNT NO. *31*

DATE		ITEM	POST. REF.	DEBIT	CREDIT	BALANCE	
						DEBIT	CREDIT

ACCOUNT *Dividends* ACCOUNT NO. *33*

DATE		ITEM	POST. REF.	DEBIT	CREDIT	BALANCE	
						DEBIT	CREDIT

ACCOUNT *Fees Earned* ACCOUNT NO. *41*

DATE		ITEM	POST. REF.	DEBIT	CREDIT	BALANCE	
						DEBIT	CREDIT

CONTINUING PROBLEM, Continued

ACCOUNT *Wages Expense* ACCOUNT NO. *50*

DATE		ITEM	POST. REF.	DEBIT	CREDIT	BALANCE DEBIT	BALANCE CREDIT

ACCOUNT *Office Rent Expense* ACCOUNT NO. *51*

DATE		ITEM	POST. REF.	DEBIT	CREDIT	BALANCE DEBIT	BALANCE CREDIT

ACCOUNT *Equipment Rent Expense* ACCOUNT NO. *52*

DATE		ITEM	POST. REF.	DEBIT	CREDIT	BALANCE DEBIT	BALANCE CREDIT

ACCOUNT *Utilities Expense* ACCOUNT NO. *53*

DATE		ITEM	POST. REF.	DEBIT	CREDIT	BALANCE DEBIT	BALANCE CREDIT

CONTINUING PROBLEM, Continued

ACCOUNT *Music Expense* ACCOUNT NO. *54*

DATE		ITEM	POST. REF.	DEBIT	CREDIT	BALANCE	
						DEBIT	CREDIT

ACCOUNT *Advertising Expense* ACCOUNT NO. *55*

DATE		ITEM	POST. REF.	DEBIT	CREDIT	BALANCE	
						DEBIT	CREDIT

ACCOUNT *Supplies Expense* ACCOUNT NO. *56*

DATE		ITEM	POST. REF.	DEBIT	CREDIT	BALANCE	
						DEBIT	CREDIT

ACCOUNT *Insurance Expense* ACCOUNT NO. *57*

DATE		ITEM	POST. REF.	DEBIT	CREDIT	BALANCE	
						DEBIT	CREDIT

(This account is not used in Chapter 2.)

CONTINUING PROBLEM, Continued

ACCOUNT *Depreciation Expense* ACCOUNT NO. *58*

DATE		ITEM	POST. REF.	DEBIT	CREDIT	BALANCE DEBIT	BALANCE CREDIT

(This account is not used in Chapter 2.)

ACCOUNT *Miscellaneous Expense* ACCOUNT NO. *59*

DATE		ITEM	POST. REF.	DEBIT	CREDIT	BALANCE DEBIT	BALANCE CREDIT

CONTINUING PROBLEM, Concluded

4.

Unadjusted Trial Balance

This Page Not Used.

EXERCISE 3-1

1. A two-year premium paid on a fire insurance policy: ____________________
2. Fees earned but not yet received: ____________________
3. Fees received but not yet earned: ____________________
4. Salary owed but not yet paid: ____________________
5. Subscriptions received in advance by a magazine publisher: ____________________
6. Supplies on hand: ____________________
7. Taxes owed but payable in the following period: ____________________
8. Utilities owed but not yet paid: ____________________

EXERCISE 3-2

Account	Answer
Accounts Receivable	Normally requires adjustment (AR).
Cash..	
Common Stock	
Interest Expense	
Interest Receivable	
Land	
Office Equipment	
Prepaid Rent	
Supplies	
Unearned Fees	
Wages Expense	

EXERCISE 3-3

JOURNAL PAGE

	DATE		DESCRIPTION	POST. REF.	DEBIT	CREDIT	
1							1
2							2
3							3
4							4

EXERCISE 3-4

____

____

EXERCISE 3-5

a. ______________________

____

____

b. ______________________

____

____

EXERCISE 3-6

a. and b.

JOURNAL PAGE

	DATE		DESCRIPTION	POST. REF.	DEBIT	CREDIT	
1							1
2							2
3							3
4							4
5							5
6							6
7							7
8							8

EXERCISE 3-7

a. and b.

JOURNAL PAGE

	DATE		DESCRIPTION	POST. REF.	DEBIT	CREDIT	
1							1
2							2
3							3
4							4
5							5
6							6
7							7
8							8

EXERCISE 3-8

JOURNAL PAGE

DATE		DESCRIPTION	POST. REF.	DEBIT	CREDIT	
1						1
2						2
3						3
4						4

EXERCISE 3-9

a. ____________________

b. ____________________

EXERCISE 3-10

a.

JOURNAL PAGE

DATE		DESCRIPTION	POST. REF.	DEBIT	CREDIT	
1						1
2						2
3						3
4						4

b. ____________________

EXERCISE 3-11

a. and b.

JOURNAL PAGE

	DATE		DESCRIPTION	POST. REF.	DEBIT	CREDIT	
1							1
2							2
3							3
4							4
5							5
6							6
7							7
8							8

EXERCISE 3-12

a. ______________________________

b. ______________________________

EXERCISE 3-13

a. and b.

JOURNAL PAGE

	DATE		DESCRIPTION	POST. REF.	DEBIT	CREDIT	
1							1
2							2
3							3
4							4
5							5
6							6
7							7
8							8
9							9
10							10

EXERCISE 3-14

____

EXERCISE 3-15

a. ______________________

b. ______________________

EXERCISE 3-16

a. ______________________

b. ______________________

EXERCISE 3-17

a.

JOURNAL PAGE

	DATE		DESCRIPTION	POST. REF.	DEBIT	CREDIT	
1							1
2							2
3							3
4							4
5							5
6							6
7							7
8							8
9							9
10							10

b. ______________________

EXERCISE 3-18

JOURNAL PAGE

	DATE		DESCRIPTION	POST. REF.	DEBIT	CREDIT	
1							1
2							2
3							3
4							4

EXERCISE 3-19

a. ____________________

b. ____________________

EXERCISE 3-20

a. ____________________

b. ____________________

EXERCISE 3-21

____

EXERCISE 3-22

a. ____________________

b. ____________________

EXERCISE 3-23

	Error (a)		Error (b)	
	Overstated	**Understated**	**Overstated**	**Understated**
1. Revenue for the year would be	$	$	$	$
2. Expenses for the year would be	$	$	$	$
3. Net income for the year would be	$	$	$	$
4. Assets at July 31 would be	$	$	$	$
5. Liabilities at July 31 would be	$	$	$	$
6. Stockholders' equity at July 31 would be......	$	$	$	$

EXERCISE 3-24

____

____

EXERCISE 3-25

a.

JOURNAL PAGE

	DATE		DESCRIPTION	POST. REF.	DEBIT	CREDIT	
1							1
2							2
3							3
4							4

b. (1) ______________________

____

____

(2) ______________________

____

____

EXERCISE 3-26

JOURNAL

PAGE

	DATE		DESCRIPTION	POST. REF.	DEBIT	CREDIT	
1							1
2							2
3							3
4							4
5							5
6							6
7							7
8							8
9							9
10							10
11							11
12							12
13							13
14							14
15							15
16							16
17							17
18							18
19							19
20							20
21							21
22							22

EXERCISE 3-27

EXERCISE 3-27, Concluded

(Optional)

Adjusted Trial Balance

EXERCISE 3-28

a. ______________________

____

b. ______________________

____

c. ______________________

____

____

____

EXERCISE 3-29

a. Dell Inc.

	AMOUNT	PERCENT

b. Hewlett-Packard Company (HP)

	AMOUNT	PERCENT

c. ______________________

____

____

____

____

____

____

____

____

____

This Page Not Used.

Name ____________________

PROBLEM 3-1 ___

1.

JOURNAL

PAGE

	DATE		DESCRIPTION	POST. REF.	DEBIT	CREDIT	
1							1
2							2
3							3
4							4
5							5
6							6
7							7
8							8
9							9
10							10
11							11
12							12
13							13
14							14
15							15
16							16
17							17
18							18
19							19
20							20
21							21
22							22
23							23
24							24

2. ____________________

This Page Not Used.

PROBLEM 3-2 ___

1.

JOURNAL

PAGE

DATE		DESCRIPTION	POST. REF.	DEBIT	CREDIT

PROBLEM 3-2 ___, Concluded

2. ____

3. ____

4. ____

PROBLEM 3-3 ___

1.

JOURNAL

PAGE

	DATE		DESCRIPTION	POST. REF.	DEBIT	CREDIT	
1							1
2							2
3							3
4							4
5							5
6							6
7							7
8							8
9							9
10							10
11							11
12							12
13							13
14							14
15							15
16							16
17							17
18							18
19							19
20							20
21							21
22							22
23							23
24							24
25							25
26							26
27							27
28							28
29							29
30							30
31							31
32							32
33							33
34							34
35							35

PROBLEM 3-3 ___, Concluded

2.

	AMOUNT

3.

	AMOUNT

4. ____

____

____

____

Name ______________________

PROBLEM 3-4 ___

JOURNAL

PAGE

DATE		DESCRIPTION	POST. REF.	DEBIT	CREDIT

PROBLEM 3-4 ___, Concluded

JOURNAL

PAGE

	DATE		DESCRIPTION	POST. REF.	DEBIT	CREDIT	
1							1
2							2
3							3
4							4
5							5
6							6
7							7
8							8
9							9
10							10
11							11
12							12
13							13
14							14
15							15
16							16
17							17
18							18
19							19
20							20
21							21
22							22
23							23
24							24
25							25
26							26
27							27
28							28
29							29
30							30
31							31
32							32
33							33
34							34
35							35
36							36

Name ______________________________

PROBLEM 3-5 ___

1.

JOURNAL

PAGE

	DATE		DESCRIPTION	POST. REF.	DEBIT	CREDIT	
1							1
2							2
3							3
4							4
5							5
6							6
7							7
8							8
9							9
10							10
11							11
12							12
13							13
14							14
15							15
16							16
17							17
18							18
19							19
20							20
21							21
22							22
23							23
24							24
25							25
26							26
27							27
28							28
29							29
30							30
31							31
32							32
33							33
34							34
35							35

PROBLEM 3-5 ___, Concluded

2.

Adjusted Trial Balance

PROBLEM 3-6 ___

1.

JOURNAL

PAGE

	DATE		DESCRIPTION	POST. REF.	DEBIT	CREDIT	
1							1
2							2
3							3
4							4
5							5
6							6
7							7
8							8
9							9
10							10
11							11
12							12
13							13
14							14
15							15
16							16
17							17
18							18
19							19
20							20

2.

	Net Income	Total Assets	=	Total Liabilities	+	Total Stockholders' Equity
Reported amounts	$	$		$		$
Corrections:						
Adjustment (a)						
Adjustment (b)						
Adjustment (c)						
Adjustment (d)						
Corrected amounts	$	$		$		$

This Page Not Used.

CONTINUING PROBLEM

1.

JOURNAL

PAGE *3*

	DATE		DESCRIPTION	POST. REF.	DEBIT	CREDIT	
1							1
2							2
3							3
4							4
5							5
6							6
7							7
8							8
9							9
10							10
11							11
12							12
13							13
14							14
15							15
16							16
17							17
18							18
19							19
20							20
21							21
22							22
23							23
24							24
25							25
26							26
27							27
28							28
29							29
30							30
31							31
32							32
33							33
34							34
35							35

CONTINUING PROBLEM, Continued

2.

GENERAL LEDGER

ACCOUNT *Cash* ACCOUNT NO. *11*

DATE		ITEM	POST. REF.	DEBIT	CREDIT	BALANCE	
						DEBIT	CREDIT

CONTINUING PROBLEM, Continued

ACCOUNT *Accounts Receivable* ACCOUNT NO. *12*

DATE		ITEM	POST. REF.	DEBIT	CREDIT	BALANCE	
						DEBIT	CREDIT

ACCOUNT *Supplies* ACCOUNT NO. *14*

DATE		ITEM	POST. REF.	DEBIT	CREDIT	BALANCE	
						DEBIT	CREDIT

ACCOUNT *Prepaid Insurance* ACCOUNT NO. *15*

DATE		ITEM	POST. REF.	DEBIT	CREDIT	BALANCE	
						DEBIT	CREDIT

ACCOUNT *Office Equipment* ACCOUNT NO. *17*

DATE		ITEM	POST. REF.	DEBIT	CREDIT	BALANCE	
						DEBIT	CREDIT

CONTINUING PROBLEM, Continued

ACCOUNT *Accumulated Depreciation—Office Equipment* ACCOUNT NO. *18*

DATE	ITEM	POST. REF.	DEBIT	CREDIT	BALANCE DEBIT	BALANCE CREDIT

ACCOUNT *Accounts Payable* ACCOUNT NO. *21*

DATE	ITEM	POST. REF.	DEBIT	CREDIT	BALANCE DEBIT	BALANCE CREDIT

ACCOUNT *Wages Payable* ACCOUNT NO. *22*

DATE	ITEM	POST. REF.	DEBIT	CREDIT	BALANCE DEBIT	BALANCE CREDIT

ACCOUNT *Unearned Revenue* ACCOUNT NO. *23*

DATE	ITEM	POST. REF.	DEBIT	CREDIT	BALANCE DEBIT	BALANCE CREDIT

CONTINUING PROBLEM, Continued

ACCOUNT *Common Stock* ACCOUNT NO. *31*

DATE		ITEM	POST. REF.	DEBIT	CREDIT	BALANCE	
						DEBIT	CREDIT

ACCOUNT *Retained Earnings* ACCOUNT NO. *32*

DATE		ITEM	POST. REF.	DEBIT	CREDIT	BALANCE	
						DEBIT	CREDIT

(This account is not used in Chapter 3.)

ACCOUNT *Dividends* ACCOUNT NO. *33*

DATE		ITEM	POST. REF.	DEBIT	CREDIT	BALANCE	
						DEBIT	CREDIT

ACCOUNT *Income Summary* ACCOUNT NO. *34*

DATE		ITEM	POST. REF.	DEBIT	CREDIT	BALANCE	
						DEBIT	CREDIT

(This account is not used in Chapter 3.)

CONTINUING PROBLEM, Continued

ACCOUNT *Fees Earned* ACCOUNT NO. *41*

DATE		ITEM	POST. REF.	DEBIT	CREDIT	BALANCE	
						DEBIT	CREDIT

ACCOUNT *Wages Expense* ACCOUNT NO. *50*

DATE		ITEM	POST. REF.	DEBIT	CREDIT	BALANCE	
						DEBIT	CREDIT

ACCOUNT *Office Rent Expense* ACCOUNT NO. *51*

DATE		ITEM	POST. REF.	DEBIT	CREDIT	BALANCE	
						DEBIT	CREDIT

CONTINUING PROBLEM, Continued

ACCOUNT *Equipment Rent Expense* ACCOUNT NO. *52*

DATE		ITEM	POST. REF.	DEBIT	CREDIT	BALANCE	
						DEBIT	CREDIT

ACCOUNT *Utilities Expense* ACCOUNT NO. *53*

DATE		ITEM	POST. REF.	DEBIT	CREDIT	BALANCE	
						DEBIT	CREDIT

ACCOUNT *Music Expense* ACCOUNT NO. *54*

DATE		ITEM	POST. REF.	DEBIT	CREDIT	BALANCE	
						DEBIT	CREDIT

ACCOUNT *Advertising Expense* ACCOUNT NO. *55*

DATE		ITEM	POST. REF.	DEBIT	CREDIT	BALANCE	
						DEBIT	CREDIT

CONTINUING PROBLEM, Continued

ACCOUNT *Supplies Expense* ACCOUNT NO. *56*

DATE		ITEM	POST. REF.	DEBIT	CREDIT	BALANCE	
						DEBIT	CREDIT

ACCOUNT *Insurance Expense* ACCOUNT NO. *57*

DATE		ITEM	POST. REF.	DEBIT	CREDIT	BALANCE	
						DEBIT	CREDIT

ACCOUNT *Depreciation Expense* ACCOUNT NO. *58*

DATE		ITEM	POST. REF.	DEBIT	CREDIT	BALANCE	
						DEBIT	CREDIT

ACCOUNT *Miscellaneous Expense* ACCOUNT NO. *59*

DATE		ITEM	POST. REF.	DEBIT	CREDIT	BALANCE	
						DEBIT	CREDIT

CONTINUING PROBLEM, Concluded

3.

Adjusted Trial Balance

This Page Not Used.

EXERCISE 4-1

1. Accounts Payable: ______________________________
2. Accounts Receivable: ______________________________
3. Cash: ______________________________
4. Dividends: ______________________________
5. Fees Earned: ______________________________
6. Supplies: ______________________________
7. Unearned Rent: ______________________________
8. Utilities Expense: ______________________________
9. Wages Expense: ______________________________
10. Wages Payable: ______________________________

EXERCISE 4-2

1. Accounts Receivable: ______________________________
2. Equipment: ______________________________
3. Fees Earned: ______________________________
4. Insurance Expense: ______________________________
5. Prepaid Advertising: ______________________________
6. Prepaid Rent: ______________________________
7. Rent Revenue: ______________________________
8. Salary Expense: ______________________________
9. Salary Payable: ______________________________
10. Supplies: ______________________________
11. Supplies Expense: ______________________________
12. Unearned Rent: ______________________________

EXERCISE 4-3

Income Statement

Retained Earnings Statement

EXERCISE 4-3, Concluded

Balance Sheet

EXERCISE 4-4

Income Statement

Retained Earnings Statement

EXERCISE 4-4, Concluded

Balance Sheet

EXERCISE 4-5

Income Statement

EXERCISE 4-6

Income Statement

Name ______________________

EXERCISE 4-7

a.

Income Statement

b.

EXERCISE 4-8

Retained Earnings Statement

EXERCISE 4-9

Retained Earnings Statement

EXERCISE 4-10

1. Accounts receivable: ________________________
2. Building: ________________________
3. Cash: ________________________
4. Equipment: ________________________
5. Prepaid Insurance: ________________________
6. Supplies: ________________________

EXERCISE 4-11

EXERCISE 4-12

Balance Sheet

EXERCISE 4-13

EXERCISE 4-13, Concluded

Balance Sheet

EXERCISE 4-14

a. Accounts Payable: ______________________

b. Accumulated Depreciation—Equipment: ______________________

c. Depreciation Expense—Equipment: ______________________

d. Equipment: ______________________

e. Common Stock: ______________________

f. Dividends: ______________________

g. Fees Earned: ______________________

h. Land: ______________________

i. Supplies: ______________________

j. Supplies Expense: ______________________

k. Wages Expense: ______________________

l. Wages Payable: ______________________

EXERCISE 4-15

____

____

____

____

____

____

____

EXERCISE 4-16

a.

JOURNAL PAGE

	DATE		DESCRIPTION	POST. REF.	DEBIT	CREDIT	
1							1
2							2
3							3
4							4
5							5
6							6
7							7

b. ______________________

Name ______________________________

EXERCISE 4-17

JOURNAL PAGE

	DATE		DESCRIPTION	POST. REF.	DEBIT	CREDIT	
1							1
2							2
3							3
4							4
5							5
6							6
7							7
8							8
9							9
10							10
11							11
12							12
13							13
14							14
15							15
16							16
17							17
18							18
19							19
20							20

EXERCISE 4-18

a. Accounts Payable: ______________________________

b. Accumulated Depreciation: ______________________________

c. Cash: ______________________________

d. Common Stock: ______________________________

e. Dividends: ______________________________

f. Depreciation Expense: ______________________________

g. Fees Earned: ______________________________

h. Office Equipment: ______________________________

i. Salaries Expense: ______________________________

j. Salaries Payable: ______________________________

k. Supplies: ______________________________

EXERCISE 4-19

Post-Closing Trial Balance

EXERCISE 4-20

1. ______________________ 6. ______________________
2. ______________________ 7. ______________________
3. ______________________ 8. ______________________
4. ______________________ 9. ______________________
5. ______________________ 10. ______________________

EXERCISE 4-21

a.

	December 31	
	Year 2	**Year 1**
Current assets	$689,663	$558,850
Current liabilities	183,607	149,147
Working capital		
Current ratio		

b. ______________________

EXERCISE 4-22

a.

	Year 2	**Year 1**
Current assets	$4,199,600	$3,794,900
Current liabilities	2,209,200	2,075,800
Working capital		
Current ratio		

b. ______________________

APPENDIX EXERCISE 4-23

1. ______________________ 6. ______________________
2. ______________________ 7. ______________________
3. ______________________ 8. ______________________
4. ______________________ 9. ______________________
5. ______________________ 10. ______________________

APPENDIX EXERCISE 4-24

	A	B	C	D	E	F	G	H	I	J	K
1	Alert Security Services Co.										
2	End-of-Period Spreadsheet (Work Sheet)										
3	For the Year Ended October 31, 2016										
4		Unadjusted				Adjusted		Income		Balance	
5		Trial Balance		Adjustments		Trial Balance		Statement		Sheet	
6	Account Title	Dr.	Cr.	Dr.	Cr.	Dr.	Cr.	Dr.	Cr.	Dr.	Cr.
7	Cash	12									
8	Accounts Receivable	90									
9	Supplies	8									
10	Prepaid Insurance	12									
11	Land	190									
12	Equipment	50									
13	Accumulated Depr.—Equip.		4								
14	Accounts Payable		36								
15	Wages Payable		0								
16	Common Stock		50								
17	Retained Earnings		210								
18	Dividends	8									
19	Fees Earned		200								
20	Wages Expense	110									
21	Rent Expense	12									
22	Insurance Expense	0									
23	Utilities Expense	6									
24	Supplies Expense	0									
25	Depreciation Expense	0									
26	Miscellaneous Expense	2									
27	Totals	500	500								
28											
29											
30											
31											

APPENDIX EXERCISE 4-25

	A	B	C	D	E	F	G	H	I	J	K
1	Alert Security Services Co.										
2	End-of-Period Spreadsheet (Work Sheet)										
3	For the Year Ended October 31, 2016										
4		Unadjusted				Adjusted		Income		Balance	
5		Trial Balance		Adjustments		Trial Balance		Statement		Sheet	
6	**Account Title**	Dr.	Cr.	Dr.	Cr.	Dr.	Cr.	Dr.	Cr.	Dr.	Cr.
7	Cash					12					
8	Accounts Receivable					103					
9	Supplies					4					
10	Prepaid Insurance					2					
11	Land					190					
12	Equipment					50					
13	Accumulated Depr.—Equip.						7				
14	Accounts Payable						36				
15	Wages Payable						1				
16	Common Stock						50				
17	Retained Earnings						210				
18	Dividends					8					
19	Fees Earned						213				
20	Wages Expense					111					
21	Rent Expense					12					
22	Insurance Expense					10					
23	Utilities Expense					6					
24	Supplies Expense					4					
25	Depreciation Expense					3					
26	Miscellaneous Expense					2					
27	Totals					517	517				
28	Net income (loss)										
29											
30											
31											

APPENDIX EXERCISE 4-26

Income Statement

Retained Earnings Statement

APPENDIX EXERCISE 4-26, Concluded

Balance Sheet

APPENDIX EXERCISE 4-27

JOURNAL PAGE

	DATE		DESCRIPTION	POST. REF.	DEBIT	CREDIT	
1							1
2							2
3							3
4							4
5							5
6							6
7							7
8							8
9							9
10							10
11							11
12							12
13							13
14							14
15							15
16							16
17							17
18							18
19							19
20							20
21							21
22							22
23							23
24							24

APPENDIX EXERCISE 4-28

JOURNAL

PAGE

DATE		DESCRIPTION	POST. REF.	DEBIT	CREDIT

PROBLEM 4-1 ___

1.

Income Statement

2.

Retained Earnings Statement

PROBLEM 4-1 ____, Continued

3.

Balance Sheet

PROBLEM 4-1 ___, Continued

4.

JOURNAL

PAGE

	DATE		DESCRIPTION	POST. REF.	DEBIT	CREDIT	
1			*Closing Entries*				1
2							2
3							3
4							4
5							5
6							6
7							7
8							8
9							9
10							10
11							11
12							12
13							13
14							14
15							15
16							16
17							17
18							18
19							19
20							20
21							21
22							22
23							23
24							24
25							25
26							26
27							27
28							28
29							29
30							30
31							31
32							32
33							33
34							34
35							35

PROBLEM 4-1 ___, Concluded

5.

Post-Closing Trial Balance

PROBLEM 4-2 ___

1.

Income Statement

Retained Earnings Statement

PROBLEM 4-2 ____, Continued

Balance Sheet

PROBLEM 4-2 ___, Concluded

2.

JOURNAL

PAGE

	DATE		DESCRIPTION	POST. REF.	DEBIT	CREDIT	
1			*Closing Entries*				1
2							2
3							3
4							4
5							5
6							6
7							7
8							8
9							9
10							10
11							11
12							12
13							13
14							14
15							15
16							16
17							17
18							18
19							19
20							20
21							21
22							22
23							23
24							24

3. ____

____

____

____

This Page Not Used.

PROBLEM 4-3 ___

1., 3., and 6.

Cash

Laundry Supplies

Prepaid Insurance

Laundry Equipment

Accumulated Depreciation

Accounts Payable

PROBLEM 4-3 ___, Continued

Wages Payable

Common Stock

Retained Earnings

Dividends

Income Summary

Laundry Revenue

PROBLEM 4-3 ___, Continued

Wages Expense

Rent Expense

Utilities Expense

Laundry Supplies Expense

Depreciation Expense

Insurance Expense

Miscellaneous Expense

PROBLEM 4-3 ___, Continued

2. Optional (Appendix)

	A	B	C	D	E	F	G	H	I	J	K
1											
2	End-of-Period Spreadsheet (Work Sheet)										
3											
4		Unadjusted				Adjusted		Income		Balance	
5		Trial Balance		Adjustments		Trial Balance		Statement		Sheet	
6	Account Title	Dr.	Cr.	Dr.	Cr.	Dr.	Cr.	Dr.	Cr.	Dr.	Cr.
7											
8											
9											
10											
11											
12											
13											
14											
15											
16											
17											
18											
19											
20											
21											
22											
23											
24											
25											
26											
27											
28											
29											
30											

PROBLEM 4-3 ___, Continued

3.

JOURNAL

PAGE

	DATE		DESCRIPTION	POST. REF.	DEBIT	CREDIT	
1			*Adjusting Entries*				1
2							2
3							3
4							4
5							5
6							6
7							7
8							8
9							9
10							10
11							11
12							12
13							13
14							14
15							15
16							16
17							17
18							18
19							19
20							20
21							21
22							22
23							23
24							24
25							25
26							26
27							27
28							28
29							29
30							30
31							31
32							32
33							33
34							34
35							35

PROBLEM 4-3 ___, Continued

4.

Adjusted Trial Balance

PROBLEM 4-3 ___, Continued

5.

Income Statement

Retained Earnings Statement

PROBLEM 4-3 ___, Continued

Balance Sheet

PROBLEM 4-3 ___, Continued

6.

JOURNAL

PAGE

	DATE		DESCRIPTION	POST. REF.	DEBIT	CREDIT	
1			*Closing Entries*				1
2							2
3							3
4							4
5							5
6							6
7							7
8							8
9							9
10							10
11							11
12							12
13							13
14							14
15							15
16							16
17							17
18							18
19							19
20							20
21							21
22							22
23							23
24							24
25							25
26							26
27							27
28							28
29							29
30							30
31							31
32							32
33							33
34							34
35							35

PROBLEM 4-3 ___, Concluded

7.

Post-Closing Trial Balance

PROBLEM 4-4 ___

1., 3., and 6.

GENERAL LEDGER

ACCOUNT *Cash* ACCOUNT NO. *11*

DATE		ITEM	POST. REF.	DEBIT	CREDIT	BALANCE DEBIT	BALANCE CREDIT

ACCOUNT *Supplies* ACCOUNT NO. *13*

DATE		ITEM	POST. REF.	DEBIT	CREDIT	BALANCE DEBIT	BALANCE CREDIT

ACCOUNT *Prepaid Insurance* ACCOUNT NO. *14*

DATE		ITEM	POST. REF.	DEBIT	CREDIT	BALANCE DEBIT	BALANCE CREDIT

ACCOUNT *Equipment* ACCOUNT NO. *16*

DATE		ITEM	POST. REF.	DEBIT	CREDIT	BALANCE DEBIT	BALANCE CREDIT

ACCOUNT *Accumulated Depreciation—Equipment* ACCOUNT NO. *17*

DATE		ITEM	POST. REF.	DEBIT	CREDIT	BALANCE DEBIT	BALANCE CREDIT

PROBLEM 4-4 ___, Continued

ACCOUNT *Trucks* ACCOUNT NO. *18*

DATE		ITEM	POST. REF.	DEBIT	CREDIT	BALANCE DEBIT	BALANCE CREDIT

ACCOUNT *Accumulated Depreciation—Trucks* ACCOUNT NO. *19*

DATE		ITEM	POST. REF.	DEBIT	CREDIT	BALANCE DEBIT	BALANCE CREDIT

ACCOUNT *Accounts Payable* ACCOUNT NO. *21*

DATE		ITEM	POST. REF.	DEBIT	CREDIT	BALANCE DEBIT	BALANCE CREDIT

ACCOUNT *Wages Payable* ACCOUNT NO. *22*

DATE		ITEM	POST. REF.	DEBIT	CREDIT	BALANCE DEBIT	BALANCE CREDIT

ACCOUNT *Common Stock* ACCOUNT NO. *31*

DATE		ITEM	POST. REF.	DEBIT	CREDIT	BALANCE DEBIT	BALANCE CREDIT

PROBLEM 4-4 ___, Continued

ACCOUNT *Retained Earnings* ACCOUNT NO. *32*

DATE		ITEM	POST. REF.	DEBIT	CREDIT	BALANCE DEBIT	BALANCE CREDIT

ACCOUNT *Dividends* ACCOUNT NO. *33*

DATE		ITEM	POST. REF.	DEBIT	CREDIT	BALANCE DEBIT	BALANCE CREDIT

ACCOUNT *Income Summary* ACCOUNT NO. *34*

DATE		ITEM	POST. REF.	DEBIT	CREDIT	BALANCE DEBIT	BALANCE CREDIT

ACCOUNT *Service Revenue* ACCOUNT NO. *41*

DATE		ITEM	POST. REF.	DEBIT	CREDIT	BALANCE DEBIT	BALANCE CREDIT

PROBLEM 4-4 ___, Continued

ACCOUNT *Wages Expense* ACCOUNT NO. *51*

DATE		ITEM	POST. REF.	DEBIT	CREDIT	BALANCE DEBIT	BALANCE CREDIT

ACCOUNT *Supplies Expense* ACCOUNT NO.

DATE		ITEM	POST. REF.	DEBIT	CREDIT	BALANCE DEBIT	BALANCE CREDIT

ACCOUNT *Rent Expense* ACCOUNT NO.

DATE		ITEM	POST. REF.	DEBIT	CREDIT	BALANCE DEBIT	BALANCE CREDIT

ACCOUNT *Depreciation Expense—Equipment* ACCOUNT NO.

DATE		ITEM	POST. REF.	DEBIT	CREDIT	BALANCE DEBIT	BALANCE CREDIT

ACCOUNT *Truck Expense* ACCOUNT NO.

DATE		ITEM	POST. REF.	DEBIT	CREDIT	BALANCE DEBIT	BALANCE CREDIT

PROBLEM 4-4 ___, Continued

ACCOUNT *Depreciation Expense—Trucks* ACCOUNT NO. *56*

DATE		ITEM	POST. REF.	DEBIT	CREDIT	BALANCE DEBIT	BALANCE CREDIT

ACCOUNT *Insurance Expense* ACCOUNT NO. *57*

DATE		ITEM	POST. REF.	DEBIT	CREDIT	BALANCE DEBIT	BALANCE CREDIT

ACCOUNT *Miscellaneous Expense* ACCOUNT NO. *59*

DATE		ITEM	POST. REF.	DEBIT	CREDIT	BALANCE DEBIT	BALANCE CREDIT

PROBLEM 4-4 ___, Continued

2. Optional (Appendix)

	A	B	C	D	E	F	G	H	I	J	K
1											
2	End-of-Period Spreadsheet (Work Sheet)										
3											
4		Unadjusted				Adjusted		Income		Balance	
5		Trial Balance		Adjustments		Trial Balance		Statement		Sheet	
6	Account Title	Dr.	Cr.	Dr.	Cr.	Dr.	Cr.	Dr.	Cr.	Dr.	Cr.
7											
8											
9											
10											
11											
12											
13											
14											
15											
16											
17											
18											
19											
20											
21											
22											
23											
24											
25											
26											
27											
28											
29											
30											
31											
32											

PROBLEM 4-4 ___, Continued

3.

JOURNAL

PAGE *26*

DATE		DESCRIPTION	POST. REF.	DEBIT	CREDIT
		Adjusting Entries			

PROBLEM 4-4 ___, Continued

4.

Adjusted Trial Balance

PROBLEM 4-4___, Continued

5.

Income Statement

Retained Earnings Statement

PROBLEM 4-4 ___, Continued

Balance Sheet

Name ______________________________

PROBLEM 4-4 ___, Continued

6.

JOURNAL

PAGE 27

DATE		DESCRIPTION	POST. REF.	DEBIT	CREDIT
		Closing Entries			

PROBLEM 4-4 ___, Concluded

7.

Post-Closing Trial Balance

Name ______________________________

PROBLEM 4-5 ___

1. and 2.

JOURNAL

PAGE *1*

DATE		DESCRIPTION	POST. REF.	DEBIT	CREDIT

PROBLEM 4-5 ___, Continued

JOURNAL

PAGE 2

DATE		DESCRIPTION	POST. REF.	DEBIT	CREDIT

PROBLEM 4-5 ___, Continued

2., 6., and 9.

GENERAL LEDGER

ACCOUNT *Cash* ACCOUNT NO. *11*

DATE		ITEM	POST. REF.	DEBIT	CREDIT	BALANCE	
						DEBIT	CREDIT

ACCOUNT *Accounts Receivable* ACCOUNT NO. *12*

DATE		ITEM	POST. REF.	DEBIT	CREDIT	BALANCE	
						DEBIT	CREDIT

PROBLEM 4-5 ___, Continued

ACCOUNT *Supplies* ACCOUNT NO. *14*

DATE		ITEM	POST. REF.	DEBIT	CREDIT	BALANCE	
						DEBIT	CREDIT

ACCOUNT *Prepaid Rent* ACCOUNT NO. *15*

DATE		ITEM	POST. REF.	DEBIT	CREDIT	BALANCE	
						DEBIT	CREDIT

ACCOUNT *Prepaid Insurance* ACCOUNT NO. *16*

DATE		ITEM	POST. REF.	DEBIT	CREDIT	BALANCE	
						DEBIT	CREDIT

ACCOUNT *Office Equipment* ACCOUNT NO. *18*

DATE		ITEM	POST. REF.	DEBIT	CREDIT	BALANCE	
						DEBIT	CREDIT

ACCOUNT *Accumulated Depreciation* ACCOUNT NO. *19*

DATE		ITEM	POST. REF.	DEBIT	CREDIT	BALANCE	
						DEBIT	CREDIT

PROBLEM 4-5 ___, Continued

ACCOUNT *Accounts Payable* ACCOUNT NO. *21*

DATE		ITEM	POST. REF.	DEBIT	CREDIT	BALANCE DEBIT	BALANCE CREDIT

ACCOUNT *Salaries Payable* ACCOUNT NO. *22*

DATE		ITEM	POST. REF.	DEBIT	CREDIT	BALANCE DEBIT	BALANCE CREDIT

ACCOUNT *Unearned Fees* ACCOUNT NO. *23*

DATE		ITEM	POST. REF.	DEBIT	CREDIT	BALANCE DEBIT	BALANCE CREDIT

ACCOUNT *Common Stock* ACCOUNT NO. *31*

DATE		ITEM	POST. REF.	DEBIT	CREDIT	BALANCE DEBIT	BALANCE CREDIT

ACCOUNT *Retained Earnings* ACCOUNT NO. *32*

DATE		ITEM	POST. REF.	DEBIT	CREDIT	BALANCE DEBIT	BALANCE CREDIT

PROBLEM 4-5 ___, Continued

ACCOUNT *Dividends* ACCOUNT NO. *33*

DATE	ITEM	POST. REF.	DEBIT	CREDIT	BALANCE	
					DEBIT	CREDIT

ACCOUNT *Income Summary* ACCOUNT NO. *34*

DATE	ITEM	POST. REF.	DEBIT	CREDIT	BALANCE	
					DEBIT	CREDIT

ACCOUNT *Fees Earned* ACCOUNT NO. *41*

DATE	ITEM	POST. REF.	DEBIT	CREDIT	BALANCE	
					DEBIT	CREDIT

ACCOUNT *Salary Expense* ACCOUNT NO. *51*

DATE	ITEM	POST. REF.	DEBIT	CREDIT	BALANCE	
					DEBIT	CREDIT

PROBLEM 4-5 ___, Continued

ACCOUNT *Rent Expense* ACCOUNT NO.

DATE		ITEM	POST. REF.	DEBIT	CREDIT	BALANCE	
						DEBIT	CREDIT

ACCOUNT *Supplies Expense* ACCOUNT NO.

DATE		ITEM	POST. REF.	DEBIT	CREDIT	BALANCE	
						DEBIT	CREDIT

ACCOUNT *Depreciation Expense* ACCOUNT NO. *54*

DATE		ITEM	POST. REF.	DEBIT	CREDIT	BALANCE	
						DEBIT	CREDIT

ACCOUNT *Insurance Expense* ACCOUNT NO. *55*

DATE		ITEM	POST. REF.	DEBIT	CREDIT	BALANCE	
						DEBIT	CREDIT

PROBLEM 4-5 ___, Continued

ACCOUNT *Miscellaneous Expense* ACCOUNT NO. *59*

DATE		ITEM	POST. REF.	DEBIT	CREDIT	BALANCE DEBIT	BALANCE CREDIT

PROBLEM 4-5 ___, Continued

3.

Unadjusted Trial Balance

PROBLEM 4-5 ___, Continued

5. Optional (Appendix)

	A	B	C	D	E	F	G	H	I	J	K
1											
2	End-of-Period Spreadsheet (Work Sheet)										
3											
4		Unadjusted				Adjusted		Income		Balance	
5		Trial Balance		Adjustments		Trial Balance		Statement		Sheet	
6	Account Title	Dr.	Cr.	Dr.	Cr.	Dr.	Cr.	Dr.	Cr.	Dr.	Cr.
7											
8											
9											
10											
11											
12											
13											
14											
15											
16											
17											
18											
19											
20											
21											
22											
23											
24											
25											
26											
27											
28											
29											
30											

Name ______________________________

PROBLEM 4-5 ___, Continued

6.

JOURNAL

PAGE *3*

DATE		DESCRIPTION	POST. REF.	DEBIT	CREDIT
		Adjusting Entries			

PROBLEM 4-5 ___, Continued

7.

Adjusted Trial Balance

PROBLEM 4-5 ___, Continued

8.

Income Statement

Retained Earnings Statement

PROBLEM 4-5 ___, Continued

Balance Sheet

PROBLEM 4-5 ___, Continued

9.

JOURNAL

PAGE *4*

DATE		DESCRIPTION	POST. REF.	DEBIT	CREDIT
		Closing Entries			

PROBLEM 4-5 ___, Concluded

10.

Post-Closing Trial Balance

CONTINUING PROBLEM

1. Optional (Appendix)

	A	B	C	D	E	F	G	H	I	J	K
1											
2	End-of-Period Spreadsheet (Work Sheet)										
3											
4		Unadjusted				Adjusted		Income		Balance	
5		Trial Balance		Adjustments		Trial Balance		Statement		Sheet	
6	Account Title	Dr.	Cr.	Dr.	Cr.	Dr.	Cr.	Dr.	Cr.	Dr.	Cr.
7											
8											
9											
10											
11											
12											
13											
14											
15											
16											
17											
18											
19											
20											
21											
22											
23											
24											
25											
26											
27											
28											
29											
30											
31											
32											
33											
34											

CONTINUING PROBLEM, Continued

2.

Income Statement

Retained Earnings Statement

CONTINUING PROBLEM, Continued

Balance Sheet

CONTINUING PROBLEM, Continued

3. Note: Use the general ledger accounts provided in Chapter 3, page 114–120.

JOURNAL

PAGE *4*

DATE		DESCRIPTION	POST. REF.	DEBIT	CREDIT
		Closing Entries			

Name ____________________________________

CONTINUING PROBLEM, Concluded

4.

Post-Closing Trial Balance

This Page Not Used.

COMPREHENSIVE PROBLEM 1

1. and 2.

JOURNAL

PAGE 5

	DATE		DESCRIPTION	POST. REF.	DEBIT	CREDIT	
1							1
2							2
3							3
4							4
5							5
6							6
7							7
8							8
9							9
10							10
11							11
12							12
13							13
14							14
15							15
16							16
17							17
18							18
19							19
20							20
21							21
22							22
23							23
24							24
25							25
26							26
27							27
28							28
29							29
30							30
31							31
32							32
33							33
34							34
35							35

COMPREHENSIVE PROBLEM 1, Continued

JOURNAL

PAGE 6

	DATE		DESCRIPTION	POST. REF.	DEBIT	CREDIT	
1							1
2							2
3							3
4							4
5							5
6							6
7							7
8							8
9							9
10							10
11							11
12							12
13							13
14							14
15							15
16							16
17							17
18							18
19							19
20							20
21							21
22							22
23							23
24							24
25							25
26							26
27							27
28							28
29							29
30							30
31							31
32							32
33							33
34							34
35							35

COMPREHENSIVE PROBLEM 1, Continued

2., 6., and 9.

GENERAL LEDGER

ACCOUNT *Cash* ACCOUNT NO. *11*

DATE	ITEM	POST. REF.	DEBIT	CREDIT	BALANCE	
					DEBIT	CREDIT

ACCOUNT *Accounts Receivable* ACCOUNT NO. *12*

DATE	ITEM	POST. REF.	DEBIT	CREDIT	BALANCE	
					DEBIT	CREDIT

COMPREHENSIVE PROBLEM 1, Continued

ACCOUNT *Supplies* ACCOUNT NO. *14*

DATE		ITEM	POST. REF.	DEBIT	CREDIT	BALANCE DEBIT	BALANCE CREDIT

ACCOUNT *Prepaid Rent* ACCOUNT NO. *15*

DATE		ITEM	POST. REF.	DEBIT	CREDIT	BALANCE DEBIT	BALANCE CREDIT

ACCOUNT *Prepaid Insurance* ACCOUNT NO. *16*

DATE		ITEM	POST. REF.	DEBIT	CREDIT	BALANCE DEBIT	BALANCE CREDIT

ACCOUNT *Office Equipment* ACCOUNT NO. *18*

DATE		ITEM	POST. REF.	DEBIT	CREDIT	BALANCE DEBIT	BALANCE CREDIT

ACCOUNT *Accumulated Depreciation* ACCOUNT NO. *19*

DATE		ITEM	POST. REF.	DEBIT	CREDIT	BALANCE DEBIT	BALANCE CREDIT

COMPREHENSIVE PROBLEM 1, Continued

ACCOUNT *Accounts Payable* ACCOUNT NO. *21*

DATE		ITEM	POST. REF.	DEBIT	CREDIT	BALANCE DEBIT	BALANCE CREDIT

ACCOUNT *Salaries Payable* ACCOUNT NO. *22*

DATE		ITEM	POST. REF.	DEBIT	CREDIT	BALANCE DEBIT	BALANCE CREDIT

ACCOUNT *Unearned Fees* ACCOUNT NO. *23*

DATE		ITEM	POST. REF.	DEBIT	CREDIT	BALANCE DEBIT	BALANCE CREDIT

ACCOUNT *Common Stock* ACCOUNT NO. *31*

DATE		ITEM	POST. REF.	DEBIT	CREDIT	BALANCE DEBIT	BALANCE CREDIT

COMPREHENSIVE PROBLEM 1, Continued

ACCOUNT *Retained Earnings* ACCOUNT NO. *32*

DATE	ITEM	POST. REF.	DEBIT	CREDIT	BALANCE	
					DEBIT	CREDIT

ACCOUNT *Dividends* ACCOUNT NO. *33*

DATE	ITEM	POST. REF.	DEBIT	CREDIT	BALANCE	
					DEBIT	CREDIT

ACCOUNT *Income Summary* ACCOUNT NO. *34*

DATE	ITEM	POST. REF.	DEBIT	CREDIT	BALANCE	
					DEBIT	CREDIT

ACCOUNT *Fees Earned* ACCOUNT NO. *41*

DATE	ITEM	POST. REF.	DEBIT	CREDIT	BALANCE	
					DEBIT	CREDIT

COMPREHENSIVE PROBLEM 1, Continued

ACCOUNT *Salary Expense* ACCOUNT NO. *51*

DATE		ITEM	POST. REF.	DEBIT	CREDIT	BALANCE DEBIT	BALANCE CREDIT

ACCOUNT *Rent Expense* ACCOUNT NO. *52*

DATE		ITEM	POST. REF.	DEBIT	CREDIT	BALANCE DEBIT	BALANCE CREDIT

ACCOUNT *Supplies Expense* ACCOUNT NO. *53*

DATE		ITEM	POST. REF.	DEBIT	CREDIT	BALANCE DEBIT	BALANCE CREDIT

ACCOUNT *Depreciation Expense* ACCOUNT NO. *54*

DATE		ITEM	POST. REF.	DEBIT	CREDIT	BALANCE DEBIT	BALANCE CREDIT

COMPREHENSIVE PROBLEM 1, Continued

ACCOUNT *Insurance Expense* ACCOUNT NO. *55*

DATE		ITEM	POST. REF.	DEBIT	CREDIT	BALANCE DEBIT	BALANCE CREDIT

ACCOUNT *Miscellaneous Expense* ACCOUNT NO. *59*

DATE		ITEM	POST. REF.	DEBIT	CREDIT	BALANCE DEBIT	BALANCE CREDIT

COMPREHENSIVE PROBLEM 1, Continued

3.

Unadjusted Trial Balance

COMPREHENSIVE PROBLEM 1, Continued

5. Optional (Appendix)

	A	B	C	D	E	F	G	H	I	J	K
1											
2	End-of-Period Spreadsheet (Work Sheet)										
3											
4		Unadjusted				Adjusted		Income		Balance	
5		Trial Balance		Adjustments		Trial Balance		Statement		Sheet	
6	Account Title	Dr.	Cr.	Dr.	Cr.	Dr.	Cr.	Dr.	Cr.	Dr.	Cr.
7											
8											
9											
10											
11											
12											
13											
14											
15											
16											
17											
18											
19											
20											
21											
22											
23											
24											
25											
26											
27											
28											
29											
30											

COMPREHENSIVE PROBLEM 1, Continued

6.

JOURNAL

PAGE 7

	DATE		DESCRIPTION	POST. REF.	DEBIT	CREDIT	
1			*Adjusting Entries*				1
2							2
3							3
4							4
5							5
6							6
7							7
8							8
9							9
10							10
11							11
12							12
13							13
14							14
15							15
16							16
17							17
18							18
19							19
20							20
21							21
22							22
23							23
24							24
25							25
26							26
27							27
28							28
29							29
30							30
31							31
32							32
33							33
34							34

COMPREHENSIVE PROBLEM 1, Continued

7.

Adjusted Trial Balance

COMPREHENSIVE PROBLEM 1, Continued

8.

Income Statement

Retained Earnings Statement

COMPREHENSIVE PROBLEM 1, Continued

Balance Sheet

COMPREHENSIVE PROBLEM 1, Continued

9.

JOURNAL

PAGE *8*

	DATE		DESCRIPTION	POST. REF.	DEBIT	CREDIT	
1			*Closing Entries*				1
2							2
3							3
4							4
5							5
6							6
7							7
8							8
9							9
10							10
11							11
12							12
13							13
14							14
15							15
16							16
17							17
18							18
19							19
20							20
21							21
22							22
23							23
24							24
25							25
26							26
27							27
28							28
29							29
30							30
31							31
32							32
33							33
34							34
35							35

COMPREHENSIVE PROBLEM 1, Concluded

10.

Post-Closing Trial Balance

EXERCISE 5-1

a. ____

b. ____

c. ____

EXERCISE 5-2

EXERCISE 5-3

a. ____

b. ____

EXERCISE 5-4

EXERCISE 5-5

(1) ______________________________

____

____

(2) ______________________________

____

____

(3) ______________________________

____

____

(4) ______________________________

____

____

EXERCISE 5-6

JOURNAL PAGE

	DATE		DESCRIPTION	POST. REF.	DEBIT	CREDIT	
1							1
2							2
3							3
4							4
5							5
6							6
7							7
8							8
9							9
10							10
11							11
12							12

EXERCISE 5-7

JOURNAL

PAGE

	DATE		DESCRIPTION	POST. REF.	DEBIT	CREDIT	
1							1
2							2
3							3
4							4
5							5
6							6
7							7
8							8
9							9
10							10
11							11
12							12
13							13
14							14
15							15
16							16
17							17
18							18
19							19
20							20
21							21
22							22
23							23
24							24

EXERCISE 5-8

JOURNAL

PAGE

	DATE		DESCRIPTION	POST. REF.	DEBIT	CREDIT	
1							1
2							2
3							3
4							4
5							5
6							6
7							7
8							8
9							9
10							10
11							11
12							12
13							13
14							14
15							15
16							16
17							17
18							18
19							19
20							20
21							21
22							22
23							23
24							24
25							25
26							26
27							27
28							28
29							29
30							30
31							31
32							32
33							33
34							34
35							35
36							36

EXERCISE 5-9

a and b.

JOURNAL PAGE

	DATE		DESCRIPTION	POST. REF.	DEBIT	CREDIT	
1							1
2							2
3							3
4							4
5							5
6							6
7							7
8							8
9							9
10							10
11							11
12							12
13							13
14							14
15							15
16							16
17							17
18							18

EXERCISE 5-10

a. ______________________

b.

JOURNAL PAGE

	DATE		DESCRIPTION	POST. REF.	DEBIT	CREDIT	
1							1
2							2
3							3
4							4
5							5
6							6
7							7
8							8

EXERCISE 5-11

(1) ______________________

____

____

(2) ______________________

____

____

(3) ______________________

____

____

(4) ______________________

____

____

(5) ______________________

____

____

EXERCISE 5-12

a. Amount of the sale: ______________________

b. Amount debited to Accounts Receivable: ______________________

c. Amount received within the discount period: ______________________

EXERCISE 5-13

	Merchandise	Freight Paid by Seller		Customer Returns and Allowances	Amount to be Paid in Full
a.	$27,000	—	FOB destination, n/30	$4,500	$__________
b.	18,600	$475	FOB shipping point, 2/10, n/30	3,000	$__________
c.	8,400	—	FOB shipping point, 1/10, n/30	700	$__________
d.	48,300	900	FOB shipping point, 2/10, n/30	6,500	$__________
e.	33,000	—	FOB destination, 1/10, n/30	—	$__________

EXERCISE 5-14

JOURNAL

PAGE

	DATE		DESCRIPTION	POST. REF.	DEBIT	CREDIT	
1							1
2							2
3							3
4							4
5							5
6							6
7							7
8							8
9							9
10							10
11							11
12							12
13							13
14							14
15							15
16							16
17							17
18							18
19							19
20							20
21							21
22							22
23							23
24							24

EXERCISE 5-15

JOURNAL

PAGE

	DATE		DESCRIPTION	POST. REF.	DEBIT	CREDIT	
1							1
2							2
3							3
4							4
5							5
6							6
7							7
8							8
9							9
10							10
11							11
12							12
13							13
14							14

EXERCISE 5-16

Balance Sheet Accounts

Acct. #	Account Name

Income Statement Accounts

Acct. #	Account Name

EXERCISE 5-17

a. ______________________

b. ______________________

c. ______________________

d. ______________________

EXERCISE 5-18

JOURNAL

PAGE

	DATE		DESCRIPTION	POST. REF.	DEBIT	CREDIT	
1							1
2							2
3							3
4							4
5							5
6							6
7							7
8							8
9							9
10							10
11							11
12							12

EXERCISE 5-19

	Debit	Credit
a. Cost of Merchandise Sold	______	______
b. Customer Refunds Payable	______	______
c. Delivery Expense.......................................	______	______
d. Estimated Returns Inventory	______	______
e. Merchandise Inventory	______	______
f. Sales..	______	______
g. Sales Tax Payable......................................	______	______

EXERCISE 5-20

a. Gross profit: ____________________

b. ____________________

____

c. ____________________

____

d. ____________________

____

EXERCISE 5-21

1. Advertising expense: ____________________

2. Depreciation expense on store equipment: ____________________

3. Insurance expense on office equipment: ____________________

4. Interest expense on notes payable: ____________________

5. Rent expense on office building: ____________________

6. Salaries of office personnel: ____________________

7. Salary of sales manager: ____________________

8. Sales supplies used: ____________________

EXERCISE 5-22

Sales	$463,400	**(b)** $________	$1,295,000	**(d)** $________
Cost of merchandise sold	**(a)** ________	410,000	**(c)** ________	900,000
Gross profit	83,500	277,500	275,000	600,000

EXERCISE 5-23

a.

Income Statement

b. ______________________

EXERCISE 5-24

(Optional)

Income Statement

EXERCISE 5-25

Income Statement

EXERCISE 5-26

JOURNAL PAGE

	DATE		DESCRIPTION	POST. REF.	DEBIT	CREDIT	
1							1
2							2
3							3
4							4
5							5

EXERCISE 5-27

a. Accounts Payable: ____________________

b. Advertising Expense: ____________________

c. Cost of Merchandise Sold: ____________________

d. Merchandise Inventory: ____________________

e. Sales: ____________________

f. Supplies: ____________________

g. Supplies Expense: ____________________

h. Valery Lavine, Drawing: ____________________

i. Wages Payable: ____________________

EXERCISE 5-28

JOURNAL PAGE

	DATE		DESCRIPTION	POST. REF.	DEBIT	CREDIT	
1			*Closing Entries*				1
2							2
3							3
4							4
5							5
6							6
7							7
8							8
9							9
10							10
11							11
12							12
13							13
14							14
15							15
16							16
17							17
18							18
19							19
20							20
21							21
22							22
23							23
24							24

EXERCISE 5-29

JOURNAL

PAGE

	DATE		DESCRIPTION	POST. REF.	DEBIT	CREDIT	
1			*Closing Entries*				1
2							2
3							3
4							4
5							5
6							6
7							7
8							8
9							9
10							10
11							11
12							12
13							13
14							14
15							15
16							16
17							17
18							18
19							19
20							20
21							21
22							22
23							23
24							24

EXERCISE 5-30

a. Year 2: ______________________

Year 1: ______________________

b. ______________________

EXERCISE 5-31

a. ____________________

b. ____________________

____

____

____

____

____

____

____

____

____

____

____

____

____

APPENDIX EXERCISE 5-32

Account	Increase	Decrease	Normal Balance
Purchases	debit	**(a)** ________	**(b)** ________
Purchase Discounts	credit	**(c)** ________	credit
Purchase Returns and Allowances	**(d)** ________	**(e)** ________	**(f)** ________
Freight In	debit	**(g)** ________	debit

APPENDIX EXERCISE 5-33

JOURNAL

PAGE

DATE		DESCRIPTION	POST. REF.	DEBIT	CREDIT

APPENDIX EXERCISE 5-34

a. Purchases – (X + Y) = Net purchases

____

b. Net purchases + X = Cost of merchandise purchased

____

c. Merchandise inventory (beginning) + Cost of merchandise purchased = X

____

d. Merchandise available for sale – X = Cost of merchandise sold

____

APPENDIX EXERCISE 5-35

a.

b. ______________________________

c. ______________________________

____

APPENDIX EXERCISE 5-36

APPENDIX EXERCISE 5-37

APPENDIX EXERCISE 5-38

(Optional)

APPENDIX EXERCISE 5-39

JOURNAL

PAGE

	DATE		DESCRIPTION	POST. REF.	DEBIT	CREDIT	
1			*Closing Entries*				1
2							2
3							3
4							4
5							5
6							6
7							7
8							8
9							9
10							10
11							11
12							12
13							13
14							14
15							15
16							16
17							17
18							18
19							19
20							20
21							21
22							22
23							23
24							24
25							25
26							26
27							27
28							28

This Page Not Used.

PROBLEM 5-1 ___

JOURNAL

PAGE

DATE		DESCRIPTION	POST. REF.	DEBIT	CREDIT

PROBLEM 5-1 ___, Concluded

JOURNAL

PAGE

	DATE		DESCRIPTION	POST. REF.	DEBIT	CREDIT	
1							1
2							2
3							3
4							4
5							5
6							6
7							7
8							8
9							9
10							10
11							11
12							12
13							13
14							14
15							15
16							16
17							17
18							18
19							19
20							20
21							21
22							22
23							23
24							24
25							25
26							26
27							27
28							28
29							29
30							30
31							31
32							32
33							33
34							34
35							35
36							36

PROBLEM 5-2 ___

JOURNAL

PAGE

	DATE		DESCRIPTION	POST. REF.	DEBIT	CREDIT	
1							1
2							2
3							3
4							4
5							5
6							6
7							7
8							8
9							9
10							10
11							11
12							12
13							13
14							14
15							15
16							16
17							17
18							18
19							19
20							20
21							21
22							22
23							23
24							24
25							25
26							26
27							27
28							28
29							29
30							30
31							31
32							32
33							33
34							34
35							35
36							36

PROBLEM 5-2 ___, Continued

JOURNAL

PAGE

	DATE		DESCRIPTION	POST. REF.	DEBIT	CREDIT	
1							1
2							2
3							3
4							4
5							5
6							6
7							7
8							8
9							9
10							10
11							11
12							12
13							13
14							14
15							15
16							16
17							17
18							18
19							19
20							20
21							21
22							22
23							23
24							24
25							25
26							26
27							27
28							28
29							29
30							30
31							31
32							32
33							33
34							34
35							35
36							36

PROBLEM 5-2 ___, Concluded

JOURNAL

PAGE

DATE		DESCRIPTION	POST. REF.	DEBIT	CREDIT

This Page Not Used.

PROBLEM 5-3 ___

JOURNAL

PAGE

	DATE		DESCRIPTION	POST. REF.	DEBIT	CREDIT	
1							1
2							2
3							3
4							4
5							5
6							6
7							7
8							8
9							9
10							10
11							11
12							12
13							13
14							14
15							15
16							16
17							17
18							18
19							19
20							20
21							21
22							22
23							23
24							24
25							25
26							26
27							27
28							28
29							29
30							30
31							31
32							32
33							33
34							34
35							35
36							36

PROBLEM 5-3 ___, Concluded

JOURNAL

PAGE

	DATE		DESCRIPTION	POST. REF.	DEBIT	CREDIT	
1							1
2							2
3							3
4							4
5							5
6							6
7							7
8							8
9							9
10							10
11							11
12							12
13							13
14							14
15							15
16							16
17							17
18							18
19							19
20							20
21							21
22							22
23							23
24							24
25							25
26							26
27							27
28							28
29							29
30							30
31							31
32							32
33							33
34							34
35							35
36							36

PROBLEM 5-4 ___

1.

JOURNAL

PAGE

DATE		DESCRIPTION	POST. REF.	DEBIT	CREDIT

PROBLEM 5-4 ___, Continued

JOURNAL

PAGE

DATE		DESCRIPTION	POST. REF.	DEBIT	CREDIT

PROBLEM 5-4 ___, Concluded

2.

JOURNAL

PAGE

	DATE		DESCRIPTION	POST. REF.	DEBIT	CREDIT	
1							1
2							2
3							3
4							4
5							5
6							6
7							7
8							8
9							9
10							10
11							11
12							12
13							13
14							14
15							15
16							16
17							17
18							18
19							19
20							20
21							21
22							22
23							23
24							24
25							25
26							26
27							27
28							28
29							29
30							30
31							31
32							32
33							33
34							34
35							35

This Page Not Used.

Name ______________________________

PROBLEM 5-5 ___

1.

Income Statement

PROBLEM 5-5 ___, Continued

2.

Retained Earnings Statement

PROBLEM 5-5 ___, Continued

3.

Balance Sheet

PROBLEM 5-5 ___, Concluded

4. a.

b.

PROBLEM 5-6 ___

1.

Income Statement

2.

Retained Earnings Statement

PROBLEM 5-6 ___, Continued

3.

Balance Sheet

PROBLEM 5-6 ___, Concluded

4.

JOURNAL

PAGE

DATE		DESCRIPTION	POST. REF.	DEBIT	CREDIT
		Closing Entries			

This Page Not Used.

APPENDIX PROBLEM 5-7 ___

JOURNAL

PAGE

DATE		DESCRIPTION	POST. REF.	DEBIT	CREDIT

APPENDIX PROBLEM 5-7 ___, Concluded

JOURNAL

PAGE

	DATE		DESCRIPTION	POST. REF.	DEBIT	CREDIT	
1							1
2							2
3							3
4							4
5							5
6							6
7							7
8							8
9							9
10							10
11							11
12							12
13							13
14							14
15							15
16							16
17							17
18							18
19							19
20							20
21							21
22							22
23							23
24							24
25							25
26							26
27							27
28							28
29							29
30							30
31							31
32							32
33							33
34							34
35							35
36							36

APPENDIX PROBLEM 5-8 ___

JOURNAL

PAGE

DATE		DESCRIPTION	POST. REF.	DEBIT	CREDIT

APPENDIX PROBLEM 5-8 ___, Concluded

JOURNAL

PAGE

DATE		DESCRIPTION	POST. REF.	DEBIT	CREDIT

APPENDIX PROBLEM 5-9 ___

1.

JOURNAL

PAGE

	DATE		DESCRIPTION	POST. REF.	DEBIT	CREDIT	
1							1
2							2
3							3
4							4
5							5
6							6
7							7
8							8
9							9
10							10
11							11
12							12
13							13
14							14
15							15
16							16
17							17
18							18
19							19
20							20
21							21
22							22
23							23
24							24
25							25
26							26
27							27
28							28
29							29
30							30
31							31
32							32
33							33
34							34
35							35

APPENDIX PROBLEM 5-9 ___, Concluded

2.

JOURNAL

PAGE

DATE		DESCRIPTION	POST. REF.	DEBIT	CREDIT

APPENDIX PROBLEM 5-10 ___

1.

2.

Income Statement

APPENDIX PROBLEM 5-10 ___, Continued

Income Statement (Continued)

APPENDIX PROBLEM 5-10 ___, Continued

3.

JOURNAL PAGE

	DATE		DESCRIPTION	POST. REF.	DEBIT	CREDIT	
1			*Closing Entries*				1
2							2
3							3
4							4
5							5
6							6
7							7
8							8
9							9
10							10
11							11
12							12
13							13
14							14
15							15
16							16
17							17
18							18
19							19
20							20
21							21
22							22
23							23
24							24
25							25
26							26
27							27
28							28
29							29
30							30
31							31
32							32
33							33
34							34
35							35

APPENDIX PROBLEM 5-10 ___, Concluded

JOURNAL

PAGE

DATE		DESCRIPTION	POST. REF.	DEBIT	CREDIT
		Closing Entries			

4. ____

____

Name ______________________________

COMPREHENSIVE PROBLEM 2

1., 2., 6., and 9.

GENERAL LEDGER

ACCOUNT *Cash* ACCOUNT NO. *110*

DATE	ITEM	POST. REF.	DEBIT	CREDIT	BALANCE DEBIT	BALANCE CREDIT

ACCOUNT *Accounts Receivable* ACCOUNT NO. *112*

DATE	ITEM	POST. REF.	DEBIT	CREDIT	BALANCE DEBIT	BALANCE CREDIT

COMPREHENSIVE PROBLEM 2, Continued

ACCOUNT *Merchandise Inventory* ACCOUNT NO. *115*

DATE	ITEM	POST. REF.	DEBIT	CREDIT	BALANCE	
					DEBIT	CREDIT

ACCOUNT *Estimated Returns Inventory* ACCOUNT NO. *116*

DATE	ITEM	POST. REF.	DEBIT	CREDIT	BALANCE	
					DEBIT	CREDIT

ACCOUNT *Prepaid Insurance* ACCOUNT NO. *117*

DATE	ITEM	POST. REF.	DEBIT	CREDIT	BALANCE	
					DEBIT	CREDIT

Name ______________________________

COMPREHENSIVE PROBLEM 2, Continued

ACCOUNT *Store Supplies* ACCOUNT NO. *118*

DATE		ITEM	POST. REF.	DEBIT	CREDIT	BALANCE DEBIT	BALANCE CREDIT

ACCOUNT *Store Equipment* ACCOUNT NO. *123*

DATE		ITEM	POST. REF.	DEBIT	CREDIT	BALANCE DEBIT	BALANCE CREDIT

ACCOUNT *Accumulated Depreciation—Store Equipment* ACCOUNT NO. *124*

DATE		ITEM	POST. REF.	DEBIT	CREDIT	BALANCE DEBIT	BALANCE CREDIT

ACCOUNT *Accounts Payable* ACCOUNT NO. *210*

DATE		ITEM	POST. REF.	DEBIT	CREDIT	BALANCE DEBIT	BALANCE CREDIT

COMPREHENSIVE PROBLEM 2, Continued

ACCOUNT *Salaries Payable* ACCOUNT NO. *211*

DATE		ITEM	POST. REF.	DEBIT	CREDIT	BALANCE	
						DEBIT	CREDIT

ACCOUNT *Customer Refunds Payable* ACCOUNT NO. *212*

DATE		ITEM	POST. REF.	DEBIT	CREDIT	BALANCE	
						DEBIT	CREDIT

ACCOUNT *Common Stock* ACCOUNT NO. *310*

DATE		ITEM	POST. REF.	DEBIT	CREDIT	BALANCE	
						DEBIT	CREDIT

ACCOUNT *Retained Earnings* ACCOUNT NO. *311*

DATE		ITEM	POST. REF.	DEBIT	CREDIT	BALANCE	
						DEBIT	CREDIT

COMPREHENSIVE PROBLEM 2, Continued

ACCOUNT *Dividends* ACCOUNT NO. *312*

DATE		ITEM	POST. REF.	DEBIT	CREDIT	BALANCE	
						DEBIT	CREDIT

ACCOUNT *Income Summary* ACCOUNT NO. *313*

DATE		ITEM	POST. REF.	DEBIT	CREDIT	BALANCE	
						DEBIT	CREDIT

ACCOUNT *Sales* ACCOUNT NO. *410*

DATE		ITEM	POST. REF.	DEBIT	CREDIT	BALANCE	
						DEBIT	CREDIT

COMPREHENSIVE PROBLEM 2, Continued

ACCOUNT *Cost of Merchandise Sold* ACCOUNT NO. *510*

DATE		ITEM	POST. REF.	DEBIT	CREDIT	BALANCE	
						DEBIT	CREDIT

ACCOUNT *Sales Salaries Expense* ACCOUNT NO. *520*

DATE		ITEM	POST. REF.	DEBIT	CREDIT	BALANCE	
						DEBIT	CREDIT

ACCOUNT *Advertising Expense* ACCOUNT NO. *521*

DATE		ITEM	POST. REF.	DEBIT	CREDIT	BALANCE	
						DEBIT	CREDIT

ACCOUNT *Depreciation Expense* ACCOUNT NO. *522*

DATE		ITEM	POST. REF.	DEBIT	CREDIT	BALANCE	
						DEBIT	CREDIT

COMPREHENSIVE PROBLEM 2, Continued

ACCOUNT *Store Supplies Expense* ACCOUNT NO. *523*

DATE		ITEM	POST. REF.	DEBIT	CREDIT	BALANCE DEBIT	BALANCE CREDIT

ACCOUNT *Miscellaneous Selling Expense* ACCOUNT NO. *529*

DATE		ITEM	POST. REF.	DEBIT	CREDIT	BALANCE DEBIT	BALANCE CREDIT

ACCOUNT *Office Salaries Expense* ACCOUNT NO. *530*

DATE		ITEM	POST. REF.	DEBIT	CREDIT	BALANCE DEBIT	BALANCE CREDIT

ACCOUNT *Rent Expense* ACCOUNT NO. *531*

DATE		ITEM	POST. REF.	DEBIT	CREDIT	BALANCE DEBIT	BALANCE CREDIT

COMPREHENSIVE PROBLEM 2, Continued

ACCOUNT *Insurance Expense* ACCOUNT NO. *532*

DATE		ITEM	POST. REF.	DEBIT	CREDIT	BALANCE DEBIT	BALANCE CREDIT

ACCOUNT *Miscellaneous Administrative Expense* ACCOUNT NO. *539*

DATE		ITEM	POST. REF.	DEBIT	CREDIT	BALANCE DEBIT	BALANCE CREDIT

COMPREHENSIVE PROBLEM 2, Continued

1. and 2.

JOURNAL

PAGE 20

	DATE		DESCRIPTION	POST. REF.	DEBIT	CREDIT	
1							1
2							2
3							3
4							4
5							5
6							6
7							7
8							8
9							9
10							10
11							11
12							12
13							13
14							14
15							15
16							16
17							17
18							18
19							19
20							20
21							21
22							22
23							23
24							24
25							25
26							26
27							27
28							28
29							29
30							30
31							31
32							32
33							33
34							34
35							35

COMPREHENSIVE PROBLEM 2, Continued

JOURNAL

PAGE 20
continued

DATE		DESCRIPTION	POST. REF.	DEBIT	CREDIT

COMPREHENSIVE PROBLEM 2, Continued

JOURNAL

PAGE *21*

DATE		DESCRIPTION	POST. REF.	DEBIT	CREDIT

COMPREHENSIVE PROBLEM 2, Continued

JOURNAL

PAGE *21*
continued

	DATE		DESCRIPTION	POST. REF.	DEBIT	CREDIT	
1							1
2							2
3							3
4							4
5							5
6							6
7							7
8							8
9							9
10							10
11							11
12							12
13							13
14							14
15							15
16							16
17							17
18							18
19							19
20							20
21							21
22							22
23							23
24							24
25							25
26							26
27							27
28							28
29							29
30							30
31							31
32							32
33							33
34							34
35							35

COMPREHENSIVE PROBLEM 2, Continued

3.

Unadjusted Trial Balance

COMPREHENSIVE PROBLEM 2, Continued

4. and 6.

JOURNAL

PAGE 22

	DATE		DESCRIPTION	POST. REF.	DEBIT	CREDIT	
1			*Adjusting Entries*				1
2							2
3							3
4							4
5							5
6							6
7							7
8							8
9							9
10							10
11							11
12							12
13							13
14							14
15							15
16							16
17							17
18							18
19							19
20							20
21							21
22							22
23							23
24							24
25							25
26							26
27							27
28							28
29							29
30							30
31							31
32							32
33							33
34							34
35							35

COMPREHENSIVE PROBLEM 2, Continued

7.

Adjusted Trial Balance

COMPREHENSIVE PROBLEM 2, Continued

8.

Income Statement

COMPREHENSIVE PROBLEM 2, Continued

Retained Earnings Statement

COMPREHENSIVE PROBLEM 2, Continued

Balance Sheet

COMPREHENSIVE PROBLEM 2, Continued

9.

JOURNAL

PAGE *23*

	DATE		DESCRIPTION	POST. REF.	DEBIT	CREDIT	
1			*Closing Entries*				1
2							2
3							3
4							4
5							5
6							6
7							7
8							8
9							9
10							10
11							11
12							12
13							13
14							14
15							15
16							16
17							17
18							18
19							19
20							20
21							21
22							22
23							23
24							24
25							25
26							26
27							27
28							28
29							29
30							30
31							31
32							32
33							33
34							34
35							35

COMPREHENSIVE PROBLEM 2, Continued

10.

Post-Closing Trial Balance

COMPREHENSIVE PROBLEM 2, Concluded

5. **(Optional)** *This work sheet is applicable only if the end-of-period spreadsheet (work sheet) is used.*

	A	B	C	D	E	F	G	H	I	J	K
1											
2	End-of-Period Spreadsheet (Work Sheet)										
3											
4		Unadjusted Trial				Adjusted Trial					
5		Balance		Adjustments		Balance		Income Statement		Balance Sheet	
6	Account Title	Dr.	Cr.	Dr.	Cr.	Dr.	Cr.	Dr.	Cr.	Dr.	Cr.
7											
8											
9											
10											
11											
12											
13											
14											
15											
16											
17											
18											
19											
20											
21											
22											
23											
24											
25											
26											
27											
28											
29											
30											
31											
32											
33											

This Page Not Used.

EXERCISE 6-1

EXERCISE 6-2

a.

b.

c.

EXERCISE 6-3

a.

Portable DVD Players									
Date	Purchases			Cost of Merchandise Sold			Inventory		
	Quantity	Unit Cost	Total Cost	Quantity	Unit Cost	Total Cost	Quantity	Unit Cost	Total Cost

b. ____

____

____

EXERCISE 6-4

Portable DVD Players									
Date	Purchases			Cost of Merchandise Sold			Inventory		
	Quantity	Unit Cost	Total Cost	Quantity	Unit Cost	Total Cost	Quantity	Unit Cost	Total Cost

EXERCISE 6-5

a.

Prepaid Cell Phones

Date	Purchases			Cost of Merchandise Sold			Inventory		
	Quantity	Unit Cost	Total Cost	Quantity	Unit Cost	Total Cost	Quantity	Unit Cost	Total Cost

b. ____________________

____

____

EXERCISE 6-6

Prepaid Cell Phones

Date	Purchases			Cost of Merchandise Sold			Inventory		
	Quantity	Unit Cost	Total Cost	Quantity	Unit Cost	Total Cost	Quantity	Unit Cost	Total Cost

EXERCISE 6-7

a. FIFO: ______________________________

____

b. LIFO: ______________________________

____

EXERCISE 6-8

Date	Purchases			Cost of Merchandise Sold			Inventory		
	Quantity	Unit Cost	Total Cost	Quantity	Unit Cost	Total Cost	Quantity	Unit Cost	Total Cost

EXERCISE 6-9

Date	Purchases			Cost of Merchandise Sold			Inventory		
	Quantity	Unit Cost	Total Cost	Quantity	Unit Cost	Total Cost	Quantity	Unit Cost	Total Cost

EXERCISE 6-10

Date	Purchases			Cost of Merchandise Sold			Inventory		
	Quantity	Unit Cost	Total Cost	Quantity	Unit Cost	Total Cost	Quantity	Unit Cost	Total Cost

EXERCISE 6-11

Date	Purchases			Cost of Merchandise Sold			Inventory		
	Quantity	Unit Cost	Total Cost	Quantity	Unit Cost	Total Cost	Quantity	Unit Cost	Total Cost

EXERCISE 6-12

a. First-in, first-out method: ______________________

b. Last-in, first-out method: ______________________

c. Weighted average cost method: ______________________

EXERCISE 6-13

Inventory Method	Cost: Merchandise Inventory	Cost: Merchandise Sold
a. First-in, first-out................................		
b. Last-in, first-out................................		
c. Weighted average cost....................		

Supporting calculations:

EXERCISE 6-14

a. 1. FIFO inventory ________ LIFO inventory

2. FIFO cost of goods sold ________ LIFO cost of goods sold

3. FIFO net income ________ LIFO net income

4. FIFO income taxes ________ LIFO income taxes

b. ____

____

____

____

____

EXERCISE 6-15

	A	B	C	D	E	F	G
1				Market		Total	
2				Value			
3	Commodity	Inventory Quantity	Cost per Unit	per Unit (Net Realizable Value)	Cost	Market	LCM
4	Ash	80	$140	$125			
5	Aspen	120	90	112			
6	Beech	30	75	74			
7	Maple	75	88	86			
8	Oak	60	140	145			
9	Total						

EXERCISE 6-16

____

____

____

____

____

____

____

EXERCISE 6-17

a.

Balance Sheet

Merchandise inventory .... ______________

Current assets .... ______________

Total assets .... ______________

Owner's equity .... ______________

b.

Income Statement

Cost of merchandise sold .... ______________

Gross profit .... ______________

Net income .... ______________

c.

Income Statement

Cost of merchandise sold .... ______________

Gross profit .... ______________

Net income .... ______________

d. ____

____

____

____

EXERCISE 6-18

a.

Balance Sheet

Merchandise inventory .... ______________________

Current assets .... ______________________

Total assets .... ______________________

Owner's equity .... ______________________

b.

Income Statement

Cost of merchandise sold .... ______________________

Gross profit .... ______________________

Net income... ______________________

c.

Income Statement

Cost of merchandise sold .... ______________________

Gross profit .... ______________________

Net income... ______________________

d. ____

____

____

____

EXERCISE 6-19

EXERCISE 6-20

a. Apple: ______________________________

American Greetings: ______________________________

b. ______________________________

EXERCISE 6-21

a. Number of Days' Sales in Inventory =

Kroger:

Safeway:

Whole Foods:

Inventory Turnover =

Kroger:

Safeway:

Whole Foods:

b.

EXERCISE 6-21, Concluded

c.

APPENDIX EXERCISE 6-22

APPENDIX EXERCISE 6-23

APPENDIX EXERCISE 6-24

APPENDIX EXERCISE 6-25

	A	B	C
1		Cost	Retail
2			
3			
4			
5			
6			
7			
8			
9			
10			

APPENDIX EXERCISE 6-26

a.

	A	B	C
1			
2			
3			
4			
5			
6			
7			
8			
9			
10			

b.

APPENDIX EXERCISE 6-27

APPENDIX EXERCISE 6-28

PROBLEM 6-1 ___

1.

Date	Purchases			Cost of Merchandise Sold			Inventory		
	Quantity	Unit Cost	Total Cost	Quantity	Unit Cost	Total Cost	Quantity	Unit Cost	Total Cost

PROBLEM 6-1 ___, Concluded

2.

JOURNAL

PAGE

	DATE		DESCRIPTION	POST. REF.	DEBIT	CREDIT	
1							1
2							2
3							3
4							4
5							5
6							6
7							7
8							8
9							9
10							10

3. ______________________________

4. ______________________________

5. ______________________________

Name ______________________________

PROBLEM 6-2 ___

1.

Date	Purchases			Cost of Merchandise Sold			Inventory		
	Quantity	Unit Cost	Total Cost	Quantity	Unit Cost	Total Cost	Quantity	Unit Cost	Total Cost

PROBLEM 6-2 ___, Continued

Date	Purchases			Cost of Merchandise Sold			Inventory		
	Quantity	Unit Cost	Total Cost	Quantity	Unit Cost	Total Cost	Quantity	Unit Cost	Total Cost

PROBLEM 6-2 ___, Concluded

2.

3. ______________________________

____

This Page Not Used.

PROBLEM 6-3 ____

Date	Purchases			Cost of Merchandise Sold			Inventory		
	Quantity	Unit Cost	Total Cost	Quantity	Unit Cost	Total Cost	Quantity	Unit Cost	Total Cost

PROBLEM 6-3 ___, Concluded

2.

3. ____

____

PROBLEM 6-4 ___

1., 2., and 3.

Inventory Method	Cost: Merchandise Inventory	Cost: Merchandise Sold
a. First-in, first-out		
b. Last-in, first-out		
c. Weighted average cost		

Supporting calculations:

PROBLEM 6-4 ___, Concluded

4.

	FIFO	LIFO	Weighted Average
Sales			
Cost of merchandise sold			
Gross profit			
Inventory, __________, 2016			

PROBLEM 6-5 ___

1.

First-In, First-Out Method

Model	Quantity	Unit Cost	Total Cost

2.

Last-In, First-Out Method

Model	Quantity	Unit Cost	Total Cost

PROBLEM 6-5 ___, Concluded

3.

Weighted Average Cost Method

Model	Quantity	Unit Cost	Total Cost

4. a. ____

b. ____

Name ______________________________

PROBLEM 6-6 ___

	A	B	C	D	E	F	G
1	Inventory Sheet						
2	December 31, 2016						
3					Total		
4							
5	Description	Inventory Quantity	Cost per Unit	Market Value per Unit (Net Realizable Value)	Cost	Market	LCM
6							
7							
8							
9							
10							
11							
12							
13							
14							
15							
16							
17							
18							
19							
20							
21							
22							
23							
24							
25							
26							
27							
28							
29							
30							
31							
32							
33							
34							
35							

This Page Not Used.

Name ______________________________

APPENDIX PROBLEM 6-7 ___

1.

	A	B	C
1			
2		**Cost**	**Retail**
3			
4			
5			
6			
7			
8			
9			
10			
11			
12			
13			
14			
15			
16			
17			
18			

2.

	A	B	C
1			
2			**Cost**
3	**a.**		
4			
5			
6			
7			
8			
9			
10			
11			
12			
13			
14			
15			
16			
17	**b.**		
18			
19			
20			
21			
22			
23			
24			

This Page Not Used.

EXERCISE 7-1

EXERCISE 7-1, Continued

EXERCISE 7-2

a.

b.

c.

EXERCISE 7-3

a.

b.

EXERCISE 7-3, Continued

c.

EXERCISE 7-3, Concluded

d. ____

EXERCISE 7-4

EXERCISE 7-5

EXERCISE 7-6

EXERCISE 7-7

EXERCISE 7-8

a. ______________________________

b. ______________________________

EXERCISE 7-9

a. ______________________________

b. ______________________________

EXERCISE 7-10

EXERCISE 7-11

a. ____

____

b. ____

____

EXERCISE 7-12

JOURNAL PAGE

	DATE		DESCRIPTION	POST. REF.	DEBIT	CREDIT	
1							1
2							2
3							3
4							4

EXERCISE 7-13

JOURNAL PAGE

	DATE		DESCRIPTION	POST. REF.	DEBIT	CREDIT	
1							1
2							2
3							3
4							4

EXERCISE 7-14

EXERCISE 7-14, Concluded

EXERCISE 7-15

EXERCISE 7-16

a. Addition to the balance per bank: ______________________

b. Deduction from the balance per bank: ______________________

c. Addition to the balance per company's records: ______________________

d. Deduction from the balance per company's records: ______________________

EXERCISE 7-17

EXERCISE 7-18

a.

Bank Reconciliation

b. ______________________

c. ______________________

EXERCISE 7-19

JOURNAL PAGE

	DATE		DESCRIPTION	POST. REF.	DEBIT	CREDIT	
1							1
2							2
3							3
4							4
5							5
6							6
7							7

EXERCISE 7-20

JOURNAL

PAGE

	DATE		DESCRIPTION	POST. REF.	DEBIT	CREDIT	
1							1
2							2
3							3
4							4

EXERCISE 7-21

a.

Bank Reconciliation

b. ____

EXERCISE 7-22

EXERCISE 7-22, Concluded

(Optional)

Bank Reconciliation

EXERCISE 7-23

a. ______________________________

Bank Reconciliation

EXERCISE 7-23, Concluded

b.

EXERCISE 7-24

a. and b.

JOURNAL PAGE

	DATE		DESCRIPTION	POST. REF.	DEBIT	CREDIT	
1							1
2							2
3							3
4							4
5							5
6							6
7							7
8							8
9							9
10							10

EXERCISE 7-25

EXERCISE 7-26

a.

b.

EXERCISE 7-27

a.

b.

c.

EXERCISE 7-28

a. Year 3: ______________________

Year 2: ______________________

Year 1: ______________________

b. Year 3: ______________________

Year 2: ______________________

Year 1: ______________________

c. ______________________

This Page Not Used.

PROBLEM 7-1 ___

This Page Not Used.

PROBLEM 7-2 ___

JOURNAL

PAGE

	DATE		DESCRIPTION	POST. REF.	DEBIT	CREDIT	
1							1
2							2
3							3
4							4
5							5
6							6
7							7
8							8
9							9
10							10
11							11
12							12
13							13
14							14
15							15
16							16
17							17
18							18
19							19
20							20
21							21
22							22
23							23
24							24
25							25
26							26
27							27
28							28
29							29
30							30
31							31
32							32
33							33
34							34
35							35
36							36

This Page Not Used.

PROBLEM 7-3 ___

1.

Bank Reconciliation

PROBLEM 7-3 ___, Concluded

2.

JOURNAL

PAGE

	DATE		DESCRIPTION	POST. REF.	DEBIT	CREDIT	
1							1
2							2
3							3
4							4
5							5
6							6
7							7
8							8
9							9
10							10

3. ____

____

____

PROBLEM 7-4 ___

1.

Bank Reconciliation

PROBLEM 7-4 ___, Concluded

2.

JOURNAL

PAGE

	DATE		DESCRIPTION	POST. REF.	DEBIT	CREDIT	
1							1
2							2
3							3
4							4
5							5
6							6
7							7
8							8
9							9
10							10
11							11
12							12
13							13
14							14
15							15
16							16
17							17
18							18
19							19
20							20

3. ____

____

____

PROBLEM 7-5 ___

1.

Bank Reconciliation

PROBLEM 7-5 ___, Concluded

2.

JOURNAL

PAGE

DATE		DESCRIPTION	POST. REF.	DEBIT	CREDIT

3. ____________________

4. ____________________

EXERCISE 8-1

EXERCISE 8-2

a. MGM Resorts International: ______________________

b. Johnson & Johnson: ______________________

c. ______________________

EXERCISE 8-3

JOURNAL

PAGE

	DATE		DESCRIPTION	POST. REF.	DEBIT	CREDIT	
1							1
2							2
3							3
4							4
5							5
6							6
7							7
8							8
9							9
10							10
11							11
12							12
13							13
14							14
15							15
16							16
17							17
18							18
19							19
20							20

EXERCISE 8-4

JOURNAL

PAGE

	DATE		DESCRIPTION	POST. REF.	DEBIT	CREDIT	
1							1
2							2
3							3
4							4
5							5
6							6
7							7
8							8
9							9
10							10
11							11
12							12
13							13
14							14
15							15
16							16
17							17
18							18
19							19
20							20
21							21
22							22

EXERCISE 8-5

a. and b.

JOURNAL

PAGE

	DATE		DESCRIPTION	POST. REF.	DEBIT	CREDIT	
1							1
2							2
3							3
4							4
5							5
6							6
7							7
8							8

EXERCISE 8-6

a. ____________________

b. ____________________

c. ____________________

d. ____________________

EXERCISE 8-7

Account	Due Date	Number of Days Past Due
Avalanche Auto	August 8	
Bales Auto	October 11	
Derby Auto Repair	June 23	
Lucky's Auto Repair	September 2	
Pit Stop Auto	September 19	
Reliable Auto Repair	July 15	
Trident Auto	August 24	
Valley Repair & Tow	May 17	

EXERCISE 8-8

a.

Customer	Due Date	Number of Days Past Due
Builders Industries	May 1	
Elkhorn Company	June 20	
Granite Creek Inc.	July 13	
Lockwood Company	September 9	
Teton Company	August 7	

EXERCISE 8-8, Concluded

b.

	A	B	C	D	E	F	G
1	Aging of Receivables Schedule						
2	August 31						
3			Not Past	Days Past Due			
4	Customer	Balance	Due	1–30	31–60	61–90	Over 90
5	Acme Industries Inc.	3,000	3,000				
6	Alliance Company	4,500		4,500			
21	Zollinger Company	5,000			5,000		
22	Subtotals	1,050,000	600,000	220,000	115,000	85,000	30,000
23							
24							
25							
26							
27							
28							
29							
30							

EXERCISE 8-9

	BALANCE	NOT PAST DUE	DAYS PAST DUE			
			1–30	31–60	61–90	OVER 90

EXERCISE 8-10

JOURNAL PAGE

	DATE		DESCRIPTION	POST. REF.	DEBIT	CREDIT	
1							1
2							2
3							3
4							4
5							5
6							6
7							7

EXERCISE 8-11

Age Interval	Balance	Estimated Uncollectible Accounts Percent	Estimated Uncollectible Accounts Amount
Not past due	$1,250,000	0.75%	$
1–30 days past due	500,000	3.00	
31–60 days past due	190,000	5.00	
61–90 days past due	60,000	15.00	
91–180 days past due	36,000	40.00	
Over 180 days past due	24,000	80.00	
Total	$2,060,000		$

EXERCISE 8-12

JOURNAL PAGE

	DATE		DESCRIPTION	POST. REF.	DEBIT	CREDIT	
1							1
2							2
3							3
4							4
5							5
6							6
7							7

Name ______________________________

EXERCISE 8-13

a.

JOURNAL

PAGE

	DATE		DESCRIPTION	POST. REF.	DEBIT	CREDIT	
1							1
2							2
3							3
4							4
5							5
6							6
7							7
8							8
9							9
10							10
11							11
12							12
13							13
14							14
15							15
16							16
17							17
18							18
19							19
20							20
21							21
22							22
23							23
24							24
25							25
26							26
27							27
28							28
29							29
30							30
31							31
32							32
33							33
34							34
35							35

EXERCISE 8-13, Continued

b.

JOURNAL

PAGE

	DATE		DESCRIPTION	POST. REF.	DEBIT	CREDIT	
1							1
2							2
3							3
4							4
5							5
6							6
7							7
8							8
9							9
10							10
11							11
12							12
13							13
14							14
15							15
16							16
17							17
18							18
19							19
20							20
21							21
22							22
23							23
24							24
25							25
26							26
27							27
28							28

EXERCISE 8-13, Concluded

c.

EXERCISE 8-14

a.

JOURNAL

PAGE

	DATE		DESCRIPTION	POST. REF.	DEBIT	CREDIT	
1							1
2							2
3							3
4							4
5							5
6							6
7							7
8							8
9							9
10							10
11							11
12							12
13							13
14							14
15							15
16							16
17							17
18							18
19							19
20							20
21							21
22							22
23							23
24							24
25							25
26							26
27							27
28							28
29							29
30							30
31							31
32							32
33							33
34							34
35							35

EXERCISE 8-14, Continued

b.

JOURNAL PAGE

	DATE		DESCRIPTION	POST. REF.	DEBIT	CREDIT	
1							1
2							2
3							3
4							4
5							5
6							6
7							7
8							8
9							9
10							10
11							11
12							12
13							13
14							14
15							15
16							16
17							17
18							18
19							19
20							20
21							21
22							22
23							23
24							24
25							25
26							26
27							27
28							28
29							29
30							30
31							31
32							32
33							33
34							34
35							35

EXERCISE 8-14, Concluded

Computations:

Aging Class (Number of Days Past Due)	Receivables Balance on December 31	Estimated Doubtful Accounts Percent	Estimated Doubtful Accounts Amount
0–30 days	$320,000	1%	$
31–60 days	110,000	3	
61–90 days	24,000	10	
91–120 days	18,000	33	
More than 120 days	43,000	75	
Total receivables	$515,000		
			$

c.

EXERCISE 8-15

EXERCISE 8-16

a. ______________________________

b. ______________________________

EXERCISE 8-17

a.

JOURNAL

PAGE

	DATE		DESCRIPTION	POST. REF.	DEBIT	CREDIT	
1							1
2							2
3							3
4							4
5							5
6							6
7							7
8							8
9							9
10							10

b.

JOURNAL

PAGE

	DATE		DESCRIPTION	POST. REF.	DEBIT	CREDIT	
1							1
2							2
3							3
4							4
5							5
6							6
7							7
8							8
9							9
10							10
11							11
12							12
13							13
14							14
15							15
16							16

EXERCISE 8-17, Concluded

c. ______________________

EXERCISE 8-18

a.

JOURNAL PAGE

	DATE		DESCRIPTION	POST. REF.	DEBIT	CREDIT	
1							1
2							2
3							3
4							4
5							5
6							6
7							7
8							8
9							9

EXERCISE 8-18, Concluded

b.

JOURNAL

PAGE

	DATE		DESCRIPTION	POST. REF.	DEBIT	CREDIT	
1							1
2							2
3							3
4							4
5							5
6							6
7							7
8							8
9							9
10							10
11							11
12							12
13							13
14							14
15							15
16							16

Computations:

Aging Class (Number of Days Past Due)	Receivables Balance on December 31	Estimated Doubtful Accounts Percent	Estimated Doubtful Accounts Amount
0–30 days	$ 715,000	1%	$
31–60 days	310,000	2	
61–90 days	102,000	15	
91–120 days	76,000	30	
More than 120 days	97,000	60	
Total receivables	$1,300,000		
			$

EXERCISE 8-18, Concluded

c. ______________________________

EXERCISE 8-19

	Date of Note	Face Amount	Interest Rate	Term of Note	Due Date	Interest Due
a.	January 3	$80,000	6%	120 days	________	$ ________
b.	February 20	27,000	4	30 days	________	________
c.	May 24	62,500	8	45 days	________	________
d.	August 30	30,000	5	90 days	________	________
e.	October 4	40,000	7	90 days	________	________

EXERCISE 8-20

a. ______________________________

b. ______________________________

c. (1) and (2)

JOURNAL

PAGE

	DATE		DESCRIPTION	POST. REF.	DEBIT	CREDIT	
1							1
2							2
3							3
4							4
5							5
6							6
7							7

EXERCISE 8-21

1. ____________________
2. ____________________
3. ____________________
4. ____________________
5. ____________________
6. ____________________
7. ____________________

EXERCISE 8-22

JOURNAL

PAGE

	DATE		DESCRIPTION	POST. REF.	DEBIT	CREDIT	
1							1
2							2
3							3
4							4
5							5
6							6
7							7
8							8
9							9
10							10
11							11
12							12
13							13
14							14
15							15
16							16
17							17
18							18
19							19
20							20
21							21
22							22

EXERCISE 8-23

JOURNAL

PAGE

	DATE		DESCRIPTION	POST. REF.	DEBIT	CREDIT	
1							1
2							2
3							3
4							4
5							5
6							6
7							7
8							8
9							9
10							10
11							11
12							12
13							13
14							14
15							15

EXERCISE 8-24

JOURNAL

PAGE

	DATE		DESCRIPTION	POST. REF.	DEBIT	CREDIT	
1							1
2							2
3							3
4							4
5							5
6							6
7							7
8							8
9							9
10							10
11							11
12							12
13							13
14							14
15							15
16							16
17							17
18							18
19							19
20							20
21							21
22							22
23							23
24							24
25							25
26							26
27							27
28							28
29							29
30							30

EXERCISE 8-25

(Optional)

Balance Sheet

EXERCISE 8-26

a. and b.

	Year 2	**Year 1**
Sales	______	______
Accounts receivable	______	______
Average accounts receivable	______	______
Accounts receivable turnover	______	______
Average daily sales	______	______
Days' sales in receivables	______	______

c. ____

EXERCISE 8-27

a. and b.

	Year 2	Year 1
Sales		
Accounts receivable		
Average accounts receivable		
Accounts receivable turnover		
Average daily sales		
Days' sales in receivables		

c. ____

EXERCISE 8-28

a. and b.

	Year 2	Year 1
Sales	________	________
Accounts receivable	________	________
Average accounts receivable	________	________
Accounts receivable turnover	________	________
Average daily sales	________	________
Days' sales in receivables	________	________

c. ____

EXERCISE 8-29

a. The Limited Brands Inc.: ____________________

H.J. Heinz Company: ____________________

b. ____________________

c. ____________________

Name ______________________________

PROBLEM 8-1 ___

1. and 2.

Allowance for Doubtful Accounts

Bad Debt Expense

3. ______________________________

4. a. ______________________________

b. ______________________________

c. ______________________________

PROBLEM 8-1 ___, Continued

2.

JOURNAL

PAGE

DATE		DESCRIPTION	POST. REF.	DEBIT	CREDIT

PROBLEM 8-1 ___, Concluded

JOURNAL

PAGE

DATE		DESCRIPTION	POST. REF.	DEBIT	CREDIT

This Page Not Used.

Name ____________________

PROBLEM 8-2 ___

1.

Customer	Due Date	Number of Days Past Due

4.

JOURNAL PAGE

	DATE		DESCRIPTION	POST. REF.	DEBIT	CREDIT	
1							1
2							2
3							3
4							4
5							5
6							6
7							7

5. ____________________

PROBLEM 8-2 ___, Concluded

2. and 3.

	A	B	C	D	E	F	G	H
1	**Aging of Receivables Schedule**							
2	**December 31, 2015**							
3			**Not Past**	**Days Past Due**				
4	**Customer**	**Balance**	**Due**	**1–30**	**31–60**	**61–90**	**91–120**	**Over 120**
5								
6								
30								
31	**Subtotals**							
32								
33								
34								
35								
36								
37								
38								
39								
40								
41								
42								
43								
44								
45								
46								

PROBLEM 8-3 ___

1.

Year	Bad Debt Expense			Balance of Allowance Account, End of Year
	Expense Actually Reported	Expense Based on Estimate	Increase (Decrease) in Amount of Expense	

2. ____

This Page Not Used.

PROBLEM 8-4 ___

1.

Note	(a) Due Date	(b) Interest Due at Maturity
1.		
2.		
3.		
4.		
5.		
6.		

2., 3., and 4.

JOURNAL

PAGE

	DATE		DESCRIPTION	POST. REF.	DEBIT	CREDIT	
1							1
2							2
3							3
4							4
5							5
6							6
7							7
8							8
9							9
10							10
11							11
12							12
13							13
14							14
15							15
16							16
17							17
18							18
19							19
20							20
21							21
22							22
23							23
24							24

This Page Not Used.

PROBLEM 8-5 ___

JOURNAL

PAGE

	DATE		DESCRIPTION	POST. REF.	DEBIT	CREDIT	
1							1
2							2
3							3
4							4
5							5
6							6
7							7
8							8
9							9
10							10
11							11
12							12
13							13
14							14
15							15
16							16
17							17
18							18
19							19
20							20
21							21
22							22
23							23
24							24
25							25
26							26
27							27
28							28
29							29
30							30
31							31
32							32
33							33
34							34
35							35
36							36

This Page Not Used.

Name ______________________

PROBLEM 8-6 ___

JOURNAL

PAGE

DATE		DESCRIPTION	POST. REF.	DEBIT	CREDIT

PROBLEM 8-6 ___, Concluded

JOURNAL

PAGE

	DATE		DESCRIPTION	POST. REF.	DEBIT	CREDIT	
1							1
2							2
3							3
4							4
5							5
6							6
7							7
8							8
9							9
10							10
11							11
12							12
13							13
14							14
15							15
16							16
17							17
18							18
19							19
20							20
21							21
22							22
23							23
24							24
25							25
26							26
27							27
28							28
29							29
30							30
31							31
32							32
33							33
34							34
35							35
36							36

EXERCISE 9-1

a. New printing press costs debited to the asset account: ______________________

b. Used printing press costs debited to the asset account: ______________________

EXERCISE 9-2

a. ______________________

b. ______________________

EXERCISE 9-3

EXERCISE 9-4

1. ____________________
2. ____________________
3. ____________________
4. ____________________
5. ____________________
6. ____________________
7. ____________________
8. ____________________
9. ____________________
10. ____________________

EXERCISE 9-5

1. ____________________
2. ____________________
3. ____________________
4. ____________________
5. ____________________
6. ____________________
7. ____________________
8. ____________________
9. ____________________
10. ____________________

EXERCISE 9-6

JOURNAL PAGE

	DATE		DESCRIPTION	POST. REF.	DEBIT	CREDIT	
1							1
2							2
3							3
4							4
5							5
6							6
7							7
8							8
9							9
10							10
11							11
12							12

EXERCISE 9-7

a. ______________________

b. ______________________

EXERCISE 9-8

a. 4 years: ______________________

b. 8 years: ______________________

c. 10 years: ______________________

d. 16 years: ______________________

e. 25 years: ______________________

f. 40 years: ______________________

g. 50 years: ______________________

EXERCISE 9-9

____

____

EXERCISE 9-10

____

____

____

____

EXERCISE 9-11

a.

Truck No.	Rate per Mile	Miles Operated	Credit to Accumulated Depreciation
1			$
2			$
3			$
4			$
Total			$

b.

JOURNAL PAGE

	DATE		DESCRIPTION	POST. REF.	DEBIT	CREDIT	
1							1
2							2
3							3
4							4
5							5

EXERCISE 9-12

a. Straight-line method:

First year: ______________________

Second year: ______________________

b. Double-declining-balance method:

First year: ______________________

Second year: ______________________

EXERCISE 9-13

a. Straight-line method:

____

b. Double-declining-balance method:

Year 1: ______________________

Year 2: ______________________

EXERCISE 9-14

a. Straight-line method:

Year 1: ______________________

Year 2: ______________________

b. Double-declining-balance method:

Year 1: ______________________

Year 2: ______________________

EXERCISE 9-15

a. ______________________

b. ______________________

c. ______________________

EXERCISE 9-16

a. and b.

JOURNAL PAGE

	DATE		DESCRIPTION	POST. REF.	DEBIT	CREDIT	
1							1
2							2
3							3
4							4
5							5
6							6
7							7
8							8
9							9
10							10

EXERCISE 9-17

a.

b. (1) and (2)

JOURNAL

PAGE

	DATE		DESCRIPTION	POST. REF.	DEBIT	CREDIT	
1							1
2							2
3							3
4							4
5							5
6							6
7							7
8							8
9							9
10							10
11							11
12							12
13							13
14							14

EXERCISE 9-18

a. 2013: ____________________

2014: ____________________

2015: ____________________

b. ____________________

EXERCISE 9-18, Concluded

c. and d.

JOURNAL PAGE

	DATE		DESCRIPTION	POST. REF.	DEBIT	CREDIT	
1							1
2							2
3							3
4							4
5							5
6							6
7							7
8							8
9							9
10							10
11							11
12							12

EXERCISE 9-19

a. ______________________________

____

b.

JOURNAL PAGE

	DATE		DESCRIPTION	POST. REF.	DEBIT	CREDIT	
1							1
2							2
3							3
4							4
5							5

EXERCISE 9-20

a.

b.

JOURNAL PAGE

	DATE		DESCRIPTION	POST. REF.	DEBIT	CREDIT	
1							1
2							2
3							3
4							4
5							5

EXERCISE 9-21

a.

	CURRENT YEAR	PRECEDING YEAR

EXERCISE 9-21, Concluded

b.

EXERCISE 9-22

EXERCISE 9-23

a.

EXERCISE 9-23, Concluded

b. ______________________

EXERCISE 9-24

a. Best Buy: ______________________

RadioShack: ______________________

b. ______________________

APPENDIX EXERCISE 9-25

a.

b.

APPENDIX EXERCISE 9-26

a.

b.

APPENDIX EXERCISE 9-27

a. and b.

JOURNAL

PAGE

	DATE		DESCRIPTION	POST. REF.	DEBIT	CREDIT	
1							1
2							2
3							3
4							4
5							5
6							6
7							7
8							8
9							9
10							10
11							11
12							12
13							13
14							14

APPENDIX EXERCISE 9-28

a. and b.

JOURNAL

PAGE

	DATE		DESCRIPTION	POST. REF.	DEBIT	CREDIT	
1							1
2							2
3							3
4							4
5							5
6							6
7							7
8							8
9							9
10							10
11							11
12							12
13							13
14							14

PROBLEM 9-1 ___

1. and 2.

Item	Land	Land Improvements	Building	Other Accounts
a.				
b.				
c.				
d.				
e.				
f.				
g.				
h.				
i.				
j.				
k.				
l.				
m.				
n.				
o.				
p.				
q.				
r.				
s.				
Total				

PROBLEM 9-1 ___, Concluded

3. ______________________

4. ______________________

PROBLEM 9-2 ___

1.

	Depreciation Expense		
Year	**a. Straight-Line Method**	**b. Units-of-Output Method**	**c. Double-Declining-Balance Method**
Total			

Supporting Calculations:

2.

3.

This Page Not Used.

PROBLEM 9-3 ___

a.

Straight-Line Method

Year	Calculations	Depreciation Expense
2014		
2015		
2016		
2017		

b.

Units-of-Output Method

Year	Calculations	Depreciation Expense
2014		
2015		
2016		
2017		

c.

Double-Declining-Balance Method

Year	Calculations	Depreciation Expense
2014		
2015		
2016		
2017		

This Page Not Used.

PROBLEM 9-4 ___

1. a.

Straight-Line Method

Year	Depreciation Expense	Accumulated Depreciation, End of Year	Book Value, End of Year
1			
2			
3			
4			
5			

b.

Double-Declining-Balance Method

Year	Depreciation Expense	Accumulated Depreciation, End of Year	Book Value, End of Year
1			
2			
3			
4			
5			

PROBLEM 9-4 ___, Concluded

2.

JOURNAL PAGE

	DATE		DESCRIPTION	POST. REF.	DEBIT	CREDIT	
1							1
2							2
3							3
4							4
5							5
6							6
7							7

3.

JOURNAL PAGE

	DATE		DESCRIPTION	POST. REF.	DEBIT	CREDIT	
1							1
2							2
3							3
4							4
5							5
6							6
7							7

PROBLEM 9-5 ___

JOURNAL

PAGE

DATE		DESCRIPTION	POST. REF.	DEBIT	CREDIT

PROBLEM 9-5 ___, Concluded

JOURNAL

PAGE

	DATE		DESCRIPTION	POST. REF.	DEBIT	CREDIT	
1							1
2							2
3							3
4							4
5							5
6							6
7							7
8							8
9							9
10							10
11							11
12							12
13							13
14							14
15							15
16							16
17							17
18							18
19							19
20							20
21							21
22							22
23							23
24							24
25							25
26							26
27							27
28							28
29							29
30							30
31							31
32							32
33							33
34							34
35							35
36							36

PROBLEM 9-6 ___

1. a. ______________________________

____

____

b. ______________________________

____

____

c. ______________________________

____

____

2.

JOURNAL

PAGE

	DATE		DESCRIPTION	POST. REF.	DEBIT	CREDIT	
1							1
2							2
3							3
4							4
5							5
6							6
7							7
8							8
9							9
10							10
11							11
12							12
13							13
14							14
15							15

This Page Not Used.

EXERCISE 10-1

EXERCISE 10-2

a. and b.

JOURNAL PAGE

	DATE		DESCRIPTION	POST. REF.	DEBIT	CREDIT	
1							1
2							2
3							3
4							4
5							5
6							6
7							7
8							8
9							9
10							10
11							11
12							12
13							13
14							14
15							15

EXERCISE 10-3

a. ____________________

b. (1) ____________________

(2) ____________________

c. ____________________

EXERCISE 10-4

a. and b.

JOURNAL PAGE

	DATE		DESCRIPTION	POST. REF.	DEBIT	CREDIT	
1							1
2							2
3							3
4							4
5							5
6							6
7							7

EXERCISE 10-5

a. and b.

JOURNAL PAGE

	DATE		DESCRIPTION	POST. REF.	DEBIT	CREDIT	
1							1
2							2
3							3
4							4
5							5
6							6
7							7

EXERCISE 10-6

a., b., and c.

JOURNAL PAGE

	DATE		DESCRIPTION	POST. REF.	DEBIT	CREDIT	
1							1
2							2
3							3
4							4
5							5
6							6
7							7
8							8
9							9
10							10
11							11
12							12
13							13
14							14
15							15

EXERCISE 10-7

a. ______________________________

____

b. ______________________________

____

c. ______________________________

____

EXERCISE 10-8

a.

b.

EXERCISE 10-9

	Consultant	Computer Programmer	Administrator
Regular earnings	$	$	$
Overtime earnings			
Gross pay	$	$	$
Less: Social security tax	$	$	$
Medicare tax			
Federal income tax withheld			
	$	$	$
Net pay	$	$	$

EXERCISE 10-9, Concluded

Withholding Supporting Calculations:

	CONSULTANT	COMPUTER PROGRAMMER	ADMINISTRATOR

EXERCISE 10-10

a.

EXERCISE 10-10, Concluded

b. and c.

JOURNAL

PAGE

	DATE		DESCRIPTION	POST. REF.	DEBIT	CREDIT	
1							1
2							2
3							3
4							4
5							5
6							6
7							7
8							8
9							9
10							10
11							11
12							12
13							13
14							14
15							15
16							16

EXERCISE 10-11

a.

EXERCISE 10-11, Concluded

b.

JOURNAL

PAGE

	DATE		DESCRIPTION	POST. REF.	DEBIT	CREDIT	
1							1
2							2
3							3
4							4
5							5
6							6
7							7
8							8
9							9

EXERCISE 10-12

a. and b.

JOURNAL

PAGE

	DATE		DESCRIPTION	POST. REF.	DEBIT	CREDIT	
1							1
2							2
3							3
4							4
5							5
6							6
7							7
8							8
9							9
10							10
11							11
12							12
13							13
14							14
15							15
16							16
17							17
18							18

EXERCISE 10-13

a. and b.

JOURNAL

PAGE

	DATE		DESCRIPTION	POST. REF.	DEBIT	CREDIT	
1							1
2							2
3							3
4							4
5							5
6							6
7							7
8							8
9							9
10							10
11							11
12							12
13							13
14							14
15							15
16							16
17							17
18							18

EXERCISE 10-14

EXERCISE 10-15

a.

b.

c.

d.

e.

EXERCISE 10-16

a.

JOURNAL PAGE

	DATE		DESCRIPTION	POST. REF.	DEBIT	CREDIT	
1							1
2							2
3							3
4							4
5							5

b. ____________________

EXERCISE 10-17

a.

JOURNAL PAGE

	DATE		DESCRIPTION	POST. REF.	DEBIT	CREDIT	
1							1
2							2
3							3
4							4
5							5
6							6
7							7
8							8

EXERCISE 10-17, Concluded

b.

EXERCISE 10-18

EXERCISE 10-19

a. and b.

JOURNAL PAGE

	DATE		DESCRIPTION	POST. REF.	DEBIT	CREDIT	
1							1
2							2
3							3
4							4
5							5
6							6
7							7
8							8
9							9
10							10

EXERCISE 10-20

a. ______________________

b.

JOURNAL PAGE

	DATE		DESCRIPTION	POST. REF.	DEBIT	CREDIT	
1							1
2							2
3							3
4							4

EXERCISE 10-20, Concluded

c.

EXERCISE 10-21

a.

JOURNAL PAGE

	DATE		DESCRIPTION	POST. REF.	DEBIT	CREDIT	
1							1
2							2
3							3
4							4
5							5

b.

EXERCISE 10-22

a. Previous year: ____________________

Current year: ____________________

b. ____________________

EXERCISE 10-23

a.

	Apple Inc:	**Dell, Inc.:**
Quick Ratio:	____________	____________

Computations:

b.

This Page Not Used.

PROBLEM 10-1 ___

1.

JOURNAL

PAGE

DATE		DESCRIPTION	POST. REF.	DEBIT	CREDIT

PROBLEM 10-1 ___, Continued

JOURNAL

PAGE

	DATE		DESCRIPTION	POST. REF.	DEBIT	CREDIT	
1							1
2							2
3							3
4							4
5							5
6							6
7							7
8							8
9							9
10							10
11							11
12							12
13							13
14							14
15							15
16							16
17							17
18							18
19							19
20							20
21							21
22							22
23							23
24							24
25							25
26							26
27							27
28							28
29							29
30							30
31							31
32							32
33							33
34							34
35							35
36							36

PROBLEM 10-1 ___, Concluded

2. a. and b.

JOURNAL

PAGE

DATE		DESCRIPTION	POST. REF.	DEBIT	CREDIT

This Page Not Used.

PROBLEM 10-2 ___

1. a. and b.

JOURNAL

PAGE

	DATE		DESCRIPTION	POST. REF.	DEBIT	CREDIT	
1							1
2							2
3							3
4							4
5							5
6							6
7							7
8							8
9							9
10							10
11							11
12							12
13							13
14							14
15							15
16							16
17							17
18							18
19							19
20							20
21							21
22							22
23							23
24							24
25							25
26							26
27							27
28							28
29							29
30							30
31							31
32							32
33							33
34							34
35							35

PROBLEM 10-2 ___, Concluded

2. a. and b.

JOURNAL

PAGE

DATE		DESCRIPTION	POST. REF.	DEBIT	CREDIT

PROBLEM 10-3 ___

1.

Employee	Gross Earnings	Federal Income Tax Withheld	Social Security Tax Withheld	Medicare Tax Withheld

PROBLEM 10-3 ___, Concluded

2. Payroll taxes incurred and paid by employer:

a. Social security tax paid by employer .... $__________

b. Medicare tax paid by employer .... __________

c. State unemployment compensation tax .... __________

Calculations and comments:

____

____

____

____

____

____

____

____

d. Federal unemployment compensation tax .... __________

e. Total payroll tax expense .... $__________

PROBLEM 10-4 ___

1.

PAYROLL FOR WEEK ENDING *December 9, 2016*

			EARNINGS			DEDUCTIONS					PAID		ACCOUNTS DEBITED		
	EMPLOYEE	TOTAL HOURS	REGULAR	OVERTIME	TOTAL	SOCIAL SECURITY TAX	MEDICARE TAX	FEDERAL INCOME TAX	U.S. SAVINGS BONDS	TOTAL	NET PAY	CK. NO.	SALES SALARIES EXPENSE	OFFICE SALARIES EXPENSE	
1															1
2															2
3															3
4															4
5															5
6															6
7															7
8															8
9															9
10															10
11															11
12															12

PROBLEM 10-4 ___, Concluded

2.

JOURNAL

PAGE

	DATE		DESCRIPTION	POST. REF.	DEBIT	CREDIT	
1							1
2							2
3							3
4							4
5							5
6							6
7							7
8							8
9							9
10							10
11							11
12							12

PROBLEM 10-5 ___

1.

JOURNAL

PAGE

	DATE	DESCRIPTION	POST. REF.	DEBIT	CREDIT	
1						1
2						2
3						3
4						4
5						5
6						6
7						7
8						8
9						9
10						10
11						11
12						12
13						13
14						14
15						15
16						16
17						17
18						18
19						19
20						20
21						21
22						22
23						23
24						24
25						25
26						26
27						27
28						28
29						29
30						30
31						31
32						32
33						33
34						34
35						35

PROBLEM 10-5 ___, Continued

JOURNAL

PAGE

	DATE		DESCRIPTION	POST. REF.	DEBIT	CREDIT	
1							1
2							2
3							3
4							4
5							5
6							6
7							7
8							8
9							9
10							10
11							11
12							12
13							13
14							14
15							15
16							16
17							17
18							18
19							19
20							20
21							21
22							22
23							23
24							24
25							25
26							26
27							27
28							28
29							29
30							30
31							31
32							32
33							33
34							34
35							35
36							36

PROBLEM 10-5 ___, Continued

JOURNAL

PAGE

	DATE		DESCRIPTION	POST. REF.	DEBIT	CREDIT	
1							1
2							2
3							3
4							4
5							5
6							6
7							7
8							8
9							9
10							10
11							11
12							12
13							13
14							14
15							15
16							16
17							17
18							18
19							19
20							20
21							21
22							22
23							23
24							24
25							25
26							26
27							27
28							28
29							29
30							30
31							31
32							32
33							33
34							34
35							35
36							36

PROBLEM 10-5 ___, Concluded

2.

JOURNAL

PAGE

DATE		DESCRIPTION	POST. REF.	DEBIT	CREDIT

COMPREHENSIVE PROBLEM 3

1.

JOURNAL

PAGE

	DATE	DESCRIPTION	POST. REF.	DEBIT	CREDIT	
1						1
2						2
3						3
4						4
5						5
6						6
7						7
8						8
9						9
10						10
11						11
12						12
13						13
14						14
15						15
16						16
17						17
18						18
19						19
20						20
21						21
22						22
23						23
24						24
25						25
26						26
27						27
28						28
29						29
30						30
31						31
32						32
33						33
34						34
35						35

COMPREHENSIVE PROBLEM 3, Continued

JOURNAL

PAGE

	DATE		DESCRIPTION	POST. REF.	DEBIT	CREDIT	
1							1
2							2
3							3
4							4
5							5
6							6
7							7
8							8
9							9
10							10
11							11
12							12
13							13
14							14
15							15
16							16
17							17
18							18
19							19
20							20
21							21
22							22
23							23
24							24
25							25
26							26
27							27
28							28
29							29
30							30
31							31
32							32
33							33
34							34
35							35
36							36

COMPREHENSIVE PROBLEM 3, Continued

JOURNAL

PAGE

	DATE		DESCRIPTION	POST. REF.	DEBIT	CREDIT	
1							1
2							2
3							3
4							4
5							5
6							6
7							7
8							8
9							9
10							10
11							11
12							12
13							13
14							14
15							15
16							16
17							17
18							18
19							19
20							20
21							21
22							22
23							23
24							24
25							25
26							26
27							27
28							28
29							29
30							30
31							31
32							32
33							33
34							34
35							35
36							36

COMPREHENSIVE PROBLEM 3, Continued

2.

Bank Reconciliation

3.

JOURNAL PAGE

	DATE		DESCRIPTION	POST. REF.	DEBIT	CREDIT	
1							1
2							2
3							3
4							4
5							5

COMPREHENSIVE PROBLEM 3, Continued

4.

JOURNAL

PAGE

DATE		DESCRIPTION	POST. REF.	DEBIT	CREDIT

COMPREHENSIVE PROBLEM 3, Continued

JOURNAL

PAGE

	DATE		DESCRIPTION	POST. REF.	DEBIT	CREDIT	
1							1
2							2
3							3
4							4
5							5
6							6
7							7
8							8
9							9
10							10
11							11
12							12
13							13
14							14
15							15
16							16
17							17
18							18
19							19
20							20
21							21
22							22
23							23
24							24
25							25
26							26
27							27
28							28
29							29
30							30
31							31
32							32
33							33
34							34
35							35
36							36

COMPREHENSIVE PROBLEM 3, Continued

5.

Balance Sheet

COMPREHENSIVE PROBLEM 3, Concluded

Balance Sheet

EXERCISE 11-1

Description	1st Year	2nd Year	3rd Year	4th Year
Total dividend declared				
Preferred dividend (current)				
Preferred dividend in arrears				
Total preferred dividends				
Preferred shares outstanding				
Preferred dividend per share				
Dividend for common shares				
Common shares outstanding				
Common dividend per share				

EXERCISE 11-2

Description	1st Year	2nd Year	3rd Year	4th Year
Total dividend declared				
Preferred dividend (current)				
Preferred dividend in arrears				
Total preferred dividends				
Preferred shares outstanding				
Preferred dividend per share				
Dividend for common shares				
Common shares outstanding				
Common dividend per share				

EXERCISE 11-3

a.

JOURNAL PAGE

	DATE		DESCRIPTION	POST. REF.	DEBIT	CREDIT	
1							1
2							2
3							3
4							4
5							5
6							6
7							7
8							8
9							9
10							10
11							11
12							12
13							13
14							14
15							15
16							16
17							17
18							18

b. ____________________

EXERCISE 11-4

a.

JOURNAL PAGE

	DATE		DESCRIPTION	POST. REF.	DEBIT	CREDIT	
1							1
2							2
3							3
4							4
5							5
6							6
7							7
8							8
9							9
10							10
11							11
12							12
13							13
14							14
15							15
16							16
17							17
18							18

b. ____

EXERCISE 11-5

JOURNAL PAGE

	DATE		DESCRIPTION	POST. REF.	DEBIT	CREDIT	
1							1
2							2
3							3
4							4
5							5
6							6
7							7
8							8
9							9

EXERCISE 11-6

a., b., and c.

JOURNAL

PAGE

	DATE		DESCRIPTION	POST. REF.	DEBIT	CREDIT	
1							1
2							2
3							3
4							4
5							5
6							6
7							7
8							8
9							9
10							10
11							11
12							12
13							13
14							14
15							15
16							16
17							17
18							18
19							19
20							20

EXERCISE 11-7

JOURNAL

PAGE

	DATE		DESCRIPTION	POST. REF.	DEBIT	CREDIT	
1							1
2							2
3							3
4							4
5							5
6							6
7							7
8							8
9							9
10							10
11							11
12							12
13							13
14							14
15							15
16							16
17							17
18							18
19							19
20							20

EXERCISE 11-8

JOURNAL

PAGE

	DATE		DESCRIPTION	POST. REF.	DEBIT	CREDIT	
1							1
2							2
3							3
4							4
5							5
6							6
7							7
8							8
9							9
10							10
11							11
12							12
13							13
14							14
15							15
16							16
17							17
18							18
19							19
20							20
21							21
22							22
23							23
24							24
25							25
26							26

EXERCISE 11-9

JOURNAL

PAGE

	DATE		DESCRIPTION	POST. REF.	DEBIT	CREDIT	
1							1
2							2
3							3
4							4
5							5
6							6
7							7
8							8
9							9

EXERCISE 11-10

a. (1) and (2)

JOURNAL

PAGE

	DATE		DESCRIPTION	POST. REF.	DEBIT	CREDIT	
1							1
2							2
3							3
4							4
5							5
6							6
7							7
8							8
9							9
10							10
11							11
12							12

b. (1) Total paid-in capital: ______________________

(2) Total retained earnings: ______________________

(3) Total stockholders' equity: ______________________

c. (1) Total paid-in capital: ______________________

(2) Total retained earnings: ______________________

(3) Total stockholders' equity: ______________________

EXERCISE 11-11

a.

JOURNAL PAGE

DATE		DESCRIPTION	POST. REF.	DEBIT	CREDIT

b. ______________________

c. ______________________

EXERCISE 11-12

a.

JOURNAL PAGE

	DATE		DESCRIPTION	POST. REF.	DEBIT	CREDIT	
1							1
2							2
3							3
4							4
5							5
6							6
7							7
8							8
9							9
10							10
11							11
12							12
13							13
14							14
15							15
16							16
17							17
18							18
19							19
20							20

b. ______________________

c. ______________________

d. ______________________

____

____

EXERCISE 11-13

a.

JOURNAL PAGE

	DATE		DESCRIPTION	POST. REF.	DEBIT	CREDIT	
1							1
2							2
3							3
4							4
5							5
6							6
7							7
8							8
9							9
10							10
11							11
12							12
13							13
14							14
15							15
16							16
17							17
18							18
19							19
20							20

b. ____

c. ____

d. ____

EXERCISE 11-14

EXERCISE 11-15

EXERCISE 11-16

EXERCISE 11-17

Retained Earnings Statement

EXERCISE 11-18

EXERCISE 11-18, Concluded

(Optional)

EXERCISE 11-19

Statement of Stockholders' Equity

EXERCISE 11-20

a. ____

b. ____

EXERCISE 11-21

	Assets	Liabilities	Stockholders' Equity
(1) Authorizing and issuing stock certificates in a stock split	________	________	________
(2) Declaring a stock dividend............................	________	________	________
(3) Issuing stock certificates for the stock dividend declared in (2)	________	________	________
(4) Declaring a cash dividend	________	________	________
(5) Paying the cash dividend declared in (4)........	________	________	________

EXERCISE 11-22

JOURNAL

PAGE

	DATE		DESCRIPTION	POST. REF.	DEBIT	CREDIT	
1							1
2							2
3							3
4							4
5							5
6							6
7							7
8							8
9							9
10							10
11							11
12							12
13							13
14							14
15							15
16							16
17							17
18							18
19							19
20							20
21							21
22							22
23							23
24							24
25							25
26							26
27							27
28							28
29							29
30							30
31							31
32							32
33							33
34							34
35							35
36							36

EXERCISE 11-23

EXERCISE 11-24

a.

EXERCISE 11-24, Concluded

b.

	YEAR 3	YEAR 2	YEAR 1

EXERCISE 11-25

a. OfficeMax: ______________________

Staples: ______________________

b. ______________________

PROBLEM 11-1 ___

1.

Year	Total Dividends	Preferred Dividends		Common Dividends	
		Total	Per Share	Total	Per Share
2011					
2012					
2013					
2014					
2015					
2016					

2. Average annual dividend for preferred: ____________________

Average annual dividend for common: ____________________

3. **a.** ____________________

b. ____________________

This Page Not Used.

Name ______________________________

PROBLEM 11-2 ___

JOURNAL

PAGE

DATE		DESCRIPTION	POST. REF.	DEBIT	CREDIT

This Page Not Used.

PROBLEM 11-3 ___

a. through g.

JOURNAL

PAGE

	DATE		DESCRIPTION	POST. REF.	DEBIT	CREDIT	
1							1
2							2
3							3
4							4
5							5
6							6
7							7
8							8
9							9
10							10
11							11
12							12
13							13
14							14
15							15
16							16
17							17
18							18
19							19
20							20
21							21
22							22
23							23
24							24
25							25
26							26
27							27
28							28
29							29
30							30
31							31
32							32
33							33
34							34
35							35

PROBLEM 11-3 ___, Concluded

JOURNAL

PAGE

DATE		DESCRIPTION	POST. REF.	DEBIT	CREDIT

PROBLEM 11-4 ___

1. and 2.

Common Stock

Paid-In Capital in Excess of Stated Value—Common Stock

Retained Earnings

Treasury Stock

PROBLEM 11-4 ___, Continued

Paid-In Capital from Sale of Treasury Stock

Stock Dividends Distributable

Stock Dividends

Cash Dividends

PROBLEM 11-4 ___, Continued

2.

JOURNAL

PAGE

	DATE		DESCRIPTION	POST. REF.	DEBIT	CREDIT	
1							1
2							2
3							3
4							4
5							5
6							6
7							7
8							8
9							9
10							10
11							11
12							12
13							13
14							14
15							15
16							16
17							17
18							18
19							19
20							20
21							21
22							22
23							23
24							24
25							25
26							26
27							27
28							28
29							29
30							30
31							31
32							32
33							33
34							34
35							35

PROBLEM 11-4 ___, Continued

JOURNAL

PAGE

DATE		DESCRIPTION	POST. REF.	DEBIT	CREDIT

PROBLEM 11-4 ___, Concluded

3.

Retained Earnings Statement

4.

This Page Not Used.

PROBLEM 11-5 ___

JOURNAL

PAGE

	DATE		DESCRIPTION	POST. REF.	DEBIT	CREDIT	
1							1
2							2
3							3
4							4
5							5
6							6
7							7
8							8
9							9
10							10
11							11
12							12
13							13
14							14
15							15
16							16
17							17
18							18
19							19
20							20
21							21
22							22
23							23
24							24
25							25
26							26
27							27
28							28
29							29
30							30
31							31
32							32
33							33
34							34
35							35
36							36

PROBLEM 11-5 ___, Concluded

JOURNAL

PAGE

	DATE		DESCRIPTION	POST. REF.	DEBIT	CREDIT	
1							1
2							2
3							3
4							4
5							5
6							6
7							7
8							8
9							9
10							10
11							11
12							12
13							13
14							14
15							15
16							16
17							17
18							18
19							19
20							20
21							21
22							22
23							23
24							24
25							25
26							26
27							27
28							28
29							29
30							30
31							31
32							32
33							33
34							34
35							35
36							36

EXERCISE 12-1

	a.	b.	c.
Earnings before bond interest and income tax	$	$	$
Less: Bond interest			
Balance	$	$	$
Less: Income tax			
Net income	$	$	$
Less: Dividends on preferred stock			
Earnings available for common stock	$	$	$
Divided by: Shares of common stock outstanding			
Earnings per share on common stock	$	$	$

EXERCISE 12-2

EXERCISE 12-3

EXERCISE 12-4

EXERCISE 12-5

JOURNAL PAGE

	DATE		DESCRIPTION	POST. REF.	DEBIT	CREDIT	
1							1
2							2
3							3
4							4
5							5
6							6
7							7
8							8
9							9

EXERCISE 12-6

a. 1. through 3.

JOURNAL PAGE

	DATE		DESCRIPTION	POST. REF.	DEBIT	CREDIT	
1							1
2							2
3							3
4							4
5							5
6							6
7							7
8							8
9							9
10							10
11							11
12							12
13							13
14							14
15							15

b.

EXERCISE 12-6, Concluded

c.

EXERCISE 12-7

a. and b.

JOURNAL PAGE

	DATE		DESCRIPTION	POST. REF.	DEBIT	CREDIT	
1							1
2							2
3							3
4							4
5							5
6							6
7							7
8							8
9							9
10							10

c.

EXERCISE 12-8

JOURNAL PAGE

	DATE		DESCRIPTION	POST. REF.	DEBIT	CREDIT	
1							1
2							2
3							3
4							4
5							5
6							6
7							7
8							8
9							9
10							10
11							11
12							12
13							13

EXERCISE 12-9

JOURNAL PAGE

	DATE		DESCRIPTION	POST. REF.	DEBIT	CREDIT	
1							1
2							2
3							3
4							4
5							5
6							6
7							7
8							8
9							9
10							10
11							11
12							12
13							13

EXERCISE 12-10

a. 1. and 2.

JOURNAL PAGE

	DATE		DESCRIPTION	POST. REF.	DEBIT	CREDIT	
1							1
2							2
3							3
4							4
5							5
6							6
7							7
8							8
9							9
10							10

b. ______________________________

EXERCISE 12-11

JOURNAL

PAGE

	DATE		DESCRIPTION	POST. REF.	DEBIT	CREDIT	
1							1
2							2
3							3
4							4
5							5
6							6
7							7
8							8
9							9
10							10
11							11
12							12
13							13
14							14
15							15

EXERCISE 12-12

a.

Amortization of Installment Notes					
	A	B	C	D	E
For the Year Ending	January 1 Carrying Amount	Note Payment (Cash Paid)	Interest Expense (7% of January 1 Note Carrying Amount)	Decrease in Notes Payable (B – C)	December 31 Carrying Amount (A – D)

EXERCISE 12-12, Concluded

b.

JOURNAL

PAGE

	DATE		DESCRIPTION	POST. REF.	DEBIT	CREDIT	
1							1
2							2
3							3
4							4
5							5
6							6
7							7
8							8
9							9
10							10
11							11
12							12
13							13
14							14
15							15
16							16
17							17
18							18
19							19
20							20
21							21
22							22
23							23
24							24
25							25

c. ____

____

EXERCISE 12-13

1.

2.

EXERCISE 12-14

a.

b.

EXERCISE 12-15

a.

b.

EXERCISE 12-16

a.

b.

APPENDIX 1 EXERCISE 12-17

a. ______________________

b. ______________________

APPENDIX 1 EXERCISE 12-18

a.

b. ______________________

c. ______________________

APPENDIX 1 EXERCISE 12-19

APPENDIX 1 EXERCISE 12-20

APPENDIX 1 EXERCISE 12-21

APPENDIX 1 EXERCISE 12-22

APPENDIX 2 EXERCISE 12-23

a. 1. through 3.

JOURNAL PAGE

	DATE		DESCRIPTION	POST. REF.	DEBIT	CREDIT	
1							1
2							2
3							3
4							4
5							5
6							6
7							7
8							8
9							9
10							10
11							11
12							12
13							13
14							14
15							15

b.

c. ______________________________

APPENDIX 2 EXERCISE 12-24

a. 1. through 3.

JOURNAL

PAGE

	DATE		DESCRIPTION	POST. REF.	DEBIT	CREDIT	
1							1
2							2
3							3
4							4
5							5
6							6
7							7
8							8
9							9
10							10
11							11
12							12
13							13
14							14
15							15

b.

c.

APPENDIX 1 AND 2 EXERCISE 12-25

a. through d.

APPENDIX 1 AND 2 EXERCISE 12-26

a. through d.

This Page Not Used.

PROBLEM 12-1 ___

1.

	Plan 1	Plan 2	Plan 3
Earnings before interest and income tax	$	$	$
Deduct: Interest on bonds			
Income before income tax	$	$	$
Deduct: Income tax			
Net income	$	$	$
Deduct: Dividends on preferred stock			
Available for dividends on common stock	$	$	$
Divided by: Shares of common stock outstanding			
Earnings per share on common stock	$	$	$

2.

	Plan 1	Plan 2	Plan 3
Earnings before interest and income tax	$	$	$
Deduct: Interest on bonds			
Income before income tax	$	$	$
Deduct: Income tax			
Net income	$	$	$
Deduct: Dividends on preferred stock			
Available for dividends on common stock	$	$	$
Divided by: Shares of common stock outstanding			
Earnings per share on common stock	$	$	$

PROBLEM 12-1 ___, Concluded

3.

PROBLEM 12-2 ___

1. and 2.

JOURNAL PAGE

	DATE		DESCRIPTION	POST. REF.	DEBIT	CREDIT	
1							1
2							2
3							3
4							4
5							5
6							6
7							7
8							8
9							9
10							10
11							11
12							12
13							13
14							14
15							15

3. ______________________

4. ______________________

5.

This Page Not Used.

Name ______________________

PROBLEM 12-3 ___

1. and 2.

JOURNAL PAGE

	DATE		DESCRIPTION	POST. REF.	DEBIT	CREDIT	
1							1
2							2
3							3
4							4
5							5
6							6
7							7
8							8
9							9
10							10
11							11
12							12
13							13
14							14
15							15

3. ______________________

4. ______________________

5.

This Page Not Used.

PROBLEM 12-4 ___

1.

JOURNAL

PAGE

	DATE		DESCRIPTION	POST. REF.	DEBIT	CREDIT	
1							1
2							2
3							3
4							4
5							5
6							6
7							7
8							8
9							9
10							10
11							11
12							12
13							13
14							14
15							15
16							16
17							17
18							18
19							19
20							20
21							21
22							22
23							23
24							24
25							25
26							26
27							27
28							28
29							29
30							30
31							31
32							32
33							33
34							34
35							35

PROBLEM 12-4 ___, Continued

JOURNAL

PAGE

DATE		DESCRIPTION	POST. REF.	DEBIT	CREDIT

PROBLEM 12-4 ___, Concluded

2. (a) 2016: ____

(b) 2017: ____

3.

This Page Not Used.

Name ______________________________

APPENDIX 1 AND 2 PROBLEM 12-5 ___

1. and 2.

JOURNAL PAGE

	DATE		DESCRIPTION	POST. REF.	DEBIT	CREDIT	
1							1
2							2
3							3
4							4
5							5
6							6
7							7
8							8
9							9
10							10
11							11
12							12
13							13
14							14
15							15
16							16
17							17
18							18
19							19
20							20

3. ____

This Page Not Used.

APPENDIX 1 AND 2 PROBLEM 12-6 ___

1. and 2.

JOURNAL

PAGE

	DATE		DESCRIPTION	POST. REF.	DEBIT	CREDIT	
1							1
2							2
3							3
4							4
5							5
6							6
7							7
8							8
9							9
10							10
11							11
12							12
13							13
14							14
15							15
16							16
17							17
18							18
19							19
20							20

3. ____

This Page Not Used.

EXERCISE 13-1

a. through d.

JOURNAL

PAGE

	DATE		DESCRIPTION	POST. REF.	DEBIT	CREDIT	
1							1
2							2
3							3
4							4
5							5
6							6
7							7
8							8
9							9
10							10
11							11
12							12
13							13
14							14
15							15
16							16
17							17
18							18
19							19
20							20
21							21
22							22
23							23
24							24
25							25

EXERCISE 13-2

a. through d.

JOURNAL

PAGE

	DATE		DESCRIPTION	POST. REF.	DEBIT	CREDIT	
1							1
2							2
3							3
4							4
5							5
6							6
7							7
8							8
9							9
10							10
11							11
12							12
13							13
14							14
15							15
16							16
17							17
18							18
19							19
20							20
21							21
22							22
23							23
24							24
25							25

EXERCISE 13-3

a. through d.

JOURNAL

PAGE

	DATE		DESCRIPTION	POST. REF.	DEBIT	CREDIT	
1							1
2							2
3							3
4							4
5							5
6							6
7							7
8							8
9							9
10							10
11							11
12							12
13							13
14							14
15							15
16							16
17							17
18							18
19							19
20							20
21							21
22							22
23							23
24							24
25							25
26							26
27							27
28							28
29							29
30							30
31							31
32							32
33							33
34							34
35							35

EXERCISE 13-4

a. and b.

JOURNAL

PAGE

DATE		DESCRIPTION	POST. REF.	DEBIT	CREDIT

EXERCISE 13-5

EXERCISE 13-6

a., b., and c.

JOURNAL PAGE

	DATE		DESCRIPTION	POST. REF.	DEBIT	CREDIT	
1							1
2							2
3							3
4							4
5							5
6							6
7							7
8							8
9							9
10							10
11							11
12							12
13							13
14							14
15							15
16							16
17							17
18							18
19							19
20							20

EXERCISE 13-7

JOURNAL

PAGE

DATE		DESCRIPTION	POST. REF.	DEBIT	CREDIT

EXERCISE 13-8

JOURNAL

PAGE

DATE		DESCRIPTION	POST. REF.	DEBIT	CREDIT

EXERCISE 13-9

JOURNAL

PAGE

DATE		DESCRIPTION	POST. REF.	DEBIT	CREDIT

EXERCISE 13-10

a.

JOURNAL

PAGE

	DATE		DESCRIPTION	POST. REF.	DEBIT	CREDIT	
1							1
2							2
3							3
4							4
5							5
6							6
7							7
8							8
9							9
10							10
11							11
12							12
13							13
14							14

b. ____

EXERCISE 13-11

a.

JOURNAL PAGE

DATE		DESCRIPTION	POST. REF.	DEBIT	CREDIT

b.

EXERCISE 13-12

a.

JOURNAL

PAGE

	DATE		DESCRIPTION	POST. REF.	DEBIT	CREDIT	
1							1
2							2
3							3
4							4
5							5
6							6
7							7
8							8
9							9
10							10
11							11
12							12
13							13
14							14
15							15
16							16
17							17
18							18

b.

EXERCISE 13-12, Concluded

c.

EXERCISE 13-13

EXERCISE 13-14

JED Capital Inc.

Selected Income Statement Items

For the Years Ended December 31, 2016 and 2017

	2016	2017
Operating income	a. ________	e. ________
Unrealized gain (loss)	b. ________	$(11,000)
Net income	c. ________	28,000

JED Capital Inc.

Selected Balance Sheet Items

December 31, 2015, 2016, and 2017

	Dec. 31, 2015	Dec. 31, 2016	Dec. 31, 2017
Trading investments, at cost	$144,000	$168,000	$205,000
Valuation allowance for trading investments	(12,000)	17,000	g. ________
Trading investments, at fair value	d. ________	f. ________	h. ________
Retained earnings	$210,000	$245,000	i. ________

EXERCISE 13-15

a.

JOURNAL

PAGE

	DATE		DESCRIPTION	POST. REF.	DEBIT	CREDIT	
1							1
2							2
3							3
4							4
5							5
6							6
7							7
8							8
9							9
10							10
11							11
12							12
13							13
14							14
15							15
16							16
17							17
18							18

b. ______________________

EXERCISE 13-16

a. and b.

JOURNAL PAGE

	DATE		DESCRIPTION	POST. REF.	DEBIT	CREDIT	
1							1
2							2
3							3
4							4
5							5
6							6
7							7
8							8
9							9
10							10
11							11
12							12
13							13
14							14
15							15
16							16
17							17
18							18

EXERCISE 13-17

a.

JOURNAL

PAGE

	DATE		DESCRIPTION	POST. REF.	DEBIT	CREDIT	
1							1
2							2
3							3
4							4
5							5
6							6
7							7

Computations:

b. ______________________

EXERCISE 13-18

a. and b.

EXERCISE 13-19

Highland Industries Inc.

Selected Income Statement Items

For the Years Ended December 31, 2016 and 2017

	2016	2017
Operating income	a. __________	g. __________
Gain (loss) from sale of investments	$7,500	$(12,000)
Net income (loss)	b. __________	(21,000)

Highland Industries Inc.

Selected Balance Sheet Items

December 31, 2015, 2016, and 2017

	Dec. 31, 2015	Dec. 31, 2016	Dec. 31, 2017
Assets			
Available-for-sale investments, at cost	$ 90,000	$ 86,000	$102,000
Valuation allowance for available-for-sale investments	12,000	(11,000)	h. __________
Available-for-sale investments, at fair value	c. __________	e. __________	i. __________
Stockholders' Equity			
Unrealized gain (loss) on available-for-sale investments	d. __________	f. __________	(16,400)
Retained earnings	$175,400	$220,000	j. __________

EXERCISE 13-20

a.

JOURNAL PAGE

	DATE		DESCRIPTION	POST. REF.	DEBIT	CREDIT	
1							1
2							2
3							3
4							4
5							5
6							6
7							7
8							8
9							9
10							10
11							11
12							12
13							13
14							14
15							15

b. ____

EXERCISE 13-21

a. 1. and 2.

JOURNAL PAGE

	DATE		DESCRIPTION	POST. REF.	DEBIT	CREDIT	
1							1
2							2
3							3
4							4
5							5
6							6
7							7
8							8
9							9
10							10
11							11
12							12
13							13
14							14
15							15

b. ______________________________

EXERCISE 13-22

a.

JOURNAL PAGE

	DATE		DESCRIPTION	POST. REF.	DEBIT	CREDIT	
1							1
2							2
3							3
4							4
5							5
6							6
7							7

Computations:

b. ______________________

EXERCISE 13-23

a.

Balance Sheet (selected items)

b.

Balance Sheet (selected items)

EXERCISE 13-24

Balance Sheet (selected Stockholders' Equity items)

EXERCISE 13-25

EXERCISE 13-26

a. Current Year: Dividend Yield: ______________________

Previous Year: Dividend Yield: ______________________

b. ______________________

EXERCISE 13-27

APPENDIX EXERCISE 13-28

APPENDIX EXERCISE 13-29

PROBLEM 13-1 ___

1.

JOURNAL PAGE

	DATE		DESCRIPTION	POST. REF.	DEBIT	CREDIT	
1							1
2							2
3							3
4							4
5							5
6							6
7							7
8							8
9							9
10							10
11							11
12							12
13							13
14							14
15							15
16							16
17							17
18							18
19							19
20							20
21							21
22							22
23							23
24							24
25							25
26							26
27							27
28							28
29							29
30							30
31							31
32							32
33							33
34							34
35							35

PROBLEM 13-1 ___, Continued

JOURNAL

PAGE

DATE		DESCRIPTION	POST. REF.	DEBIT	CREDIT

PROBLEM 13-1 ___, Concluded

2.

This Page Not Used.

PROBLEM 13-2 ___

1.

JOURNAL

PAGE

	DATE		DESCRIPTION	POST. REF.	DEBIT	CREDIT	
1							1
2							2
3							3
4							4
5							5
6							6
7							7
8							8
9							9
10							10
11							11
12							12
13							13
14							14
15							15
16							16
17							17
18							18
19							19
20							20
21							21
22							22
23							23
24							24
25							25
26							26

Calculations:

PROBLEM 13-2 ___, Continued

JOURNAL

PAGE

	DATE		DESCRIPTION	POST. REF.	DEBIT	CREDIT	
1							1
2							2
3							3
4							4
5							5
6							6
7							7
8							8
9							9
10							10
11							11
12							12
13							13
14							14
15							15
16							16
17							17
18							18
19							19
20							20
21							21
22							22
23							23
24							24
25							25
26							26
27							27
28							28
29							29
30							30
31							31
32							32
33							33
34							34
35							35
36							36

PROBLEM 13-2 ___, Concluded

2.

Balance Sheet (selected items)

3.

This Page Not Used.

PROBLEM 13-3 ___

1.

JOURNAL

PAGE

	DATE		DESCRIPTION	POST. REF.	DEBIT	CREDIT	
1							1
2							2
3							3
4							4
5							5
6							6
7							7
8							8
9							9
10							10
11							11
12							12
13							13
14							14
15							15
16							16
17							17
18							18
19							19
20							20
21							21
22							22
23							23
24							24
25							25
26							26
27							27
28							28
29							29
30							30
31							31
32							32
33							33
34							34
35							35

PROBLEM 13-3 ___, Continued

JOURNAL

PAGE

	DATE		DESCRIPTION	POST. REF.	DEBIT	CREDIT	
1							1
2							2
3							3
4							4
5							5
6							6
7							7
8							8
9							9
10							10
11							11
12							12
13							13
14							14
15							15
16							16
17							17
18							18
19							19
20							20
21							21
22							22
23							23
24							24
25							25
26							26
27							27
28							28
29							29
30							30
31							31
32							32
33							33
34							34
35							35
36							36

PROBLEM 13-3 ___, Concluded

2.

Balance Sheet (selected items)

This Page Not Used.

PROBLEM 13-4 ___

a. ______________________

b. ______________________

c. ______________________

d. ______________________

e. ______________________

f. ______________________

g. ______________________

h. ______________________

i. ______________________

Calculations:

PROBLEM 13-4 ___, Continued

Completed comparative unclassified balance sheet (optional):

Balance Sheet

	DEC. 31, 2017	DEC. 31, 2016

PROBLEM 13-4 ___, Concluded

Calculations:

This Page Not Used.

COMPREHENSIVE PROBLEM 4

1.

JOURNAL

PAGE

DATE		DESCRIPTION	POST. REF.	DEBIT	CREDIT

COMPREHENSIVE PROBLEM 4, Continued

JOURNAL

PAGE

DATE		DESCRIPTION	POST. REF.	DEBIT	CREDIT

COMPREHENSIVE PROBLEM 4, Continued

JOURNAL

PAGE

DATE		DESCRIPTION	POST. REF.	DEBIT	CREDIT

COMPREHENSIVE PROBLEM 4, Continued

JOURNAL

PAGE

DATE		DESCRIPTION	POST. REF.	DEBIT	CREDIT

COMPREHENSIVE PROBLEM 4, Continued

2. a.

Income Statement

COMPREHENSIVE PROBLEM 4, Continued

Income Statement (continued)

COMPREHENSIVE PROBLEM 4, Continued

b.

Retained Earnings Statement

COMPREHENSIVE PROBLEM 4, Continued

c.

Balance Sheet

COMPREHENSIVE PROBLEM 4, Continued

Balance Sheet (continued)

COMPREHENSIVE PROBLEM 4, Concluded

Balance Sheet (continued)

EXERCISE 14-1

EXERCISE 14-2

a.

b.

c.

d.

e.

f.

g.

h.

EXERCISE 14-3

a. Net income:

b. Paid cash dividends:

c. Issued common stock:

d. Issued bonds:

e. Redeemed bonds:

f. Sold long-term investments:

g. Purchased treasury stock:

h. Sold equipment:

i. Issued preferred stock:

j. Purchased buildings:

k. Purchased patents:

EXERCISE 14-4

a. Decrease in merchandise inventory: ____________________

b. Increase in accounts receivable: ____________________

c. Increase in accounts payable: ____________________

d. Loss on retirement of long-term debt: ____________________

e. Depreciation of fixed assets: ____________________

f. Decrease in notes receivable due in 60 days from customers: ____________________

g. Increase in salaries payable: ____________________

h. Decrease in prepaid expenses: ____________________

i. Amortization of patent: ____________________

j. Increase in notes payable due in 120 days to vendors: ____________________

k. Gain on disposal of fixed assets: ____________________

EXERCISE 14-5

a.

EXERCISE 14-5, Concluded

b.

EXERCISE 14-6

a.

EXERCISE 14-6, Concluded

b.

EXERCISE 14-7

a.

EXERCISE 14-7, Concluded

b.

EXERCISE 14-8

EXERCISE 14-9

EXERCISE 14-10

EXERCISE 14-11

EXERCISE 14-12

Name ______________________________

EXERCISE 14-13

EXERCISE 14-14

EXERCISE 14-15

a.

b.

EXERCISE 14-16

a.

Cash Flows from Operating Activities

b. ______________________

EXERCISE 14-17

a.

Statement of Cash Flows

EXERCISE 14-17, Concluded

b. ____________________

EXERCISE 14-18

EXERCISE 14-18, Continued

(Optional)

Statement of Cash Flows

EXERCISE 14-18, Concluded

Statement of Cash Flows (continued)

EXERCISE 14-19

a.

b.

c. ______________________

EXERCISE 14-20

EXERCISE 14-21

a.

b.

EXERCISE 14-22

a.

Computations:

EXERCISE 14-22, Concluded

b.

EXERCISE 14-23

Computations:

EXERCISE 14-24

a.

b. ______________________________

EXERCISE 14-25

a.

	RECENT FISCAL YEAR END (all numbers in thousands)

EXERCISE 14-25, Concluded

b.

c.

EXERCISE 14-26

This Page Not Used.

PROBLEM 14-1 ___

Statement of Cash Flows

PROBLEM 14-1 ___, Continued

Statement of Cash Flows (continued)

PROBLEM 14-1 ___, Continued

The use of this form is not required unless so indicated by the instructor.

	A	B	C	D	E
1					
2	**Spreadsheet (Work Sheet) for Statement of Cash Flows**				
3					
4		**Balance,**	**Transactions**		**Balance,**
5	**Account Title**	______	**Debit**	**Credit**	______
6					
7					
8					
9					
10					
11					
12					
13					
14					
15					
16					
17					
18					
19					
20					
21					
22					
23					
24					
25					
26					
27					
28					
29					
30					
31					
32					
33					
34					
35					
36					
37					
38					
39					
40					
41					
42					
43					
44					
45					

PROBLEM 14-1 ___, Concluded

	A	B	C	D	E
1					
2	Spreadsheet (Work Sheet) for Statement of Cash Flows (continued)				
3					
4		Balance,	Transactions		Balance,
5	Account Title		Debit	Credit	
6					
7					
8					
9					
10					
11					
12					
13					
14					
15					
16					
17					
18					
19					
20					
21					
22					
23					
24					
25					
26					
27					
28					
29					
30					
31					
32					
33					
34					
35					
36					
37					
38					
39					
40					
41					
42					
43					
44					
45					

PROBLEM 14-2 ___

Statement of Cash Flows

PROBLEM 14-2 ___, Continued

Statement of Cash Flows (continued)

PROBLEM 14-2 ___, Continued

The use of this form is not required unless so indicated by the instructor.

	A	B	C	D	E
1					
2	**Spreadsheet (Work Sheet) for Statement of Cash Flows**				
3					
4		**Balance,**	**Transactions**		**Balance,**
5	**Account Title**	________	**Debit**	**Credit**	________
6					
7					
8					
9					
10					
11					
12					
13					
14					
15					
16					
17					
18					
19					
20					
21					
22					
23					
24					
25					
26					
27					
28					
29					
30					
31					
32					
33					
34					
35					
36					
37					
38					
39					
40					
41					
42					
43					
44					
45					

PROBLEM 14-2 ___, Concluded

	A	B	C	D	E
1					
2	Spreadsheet (Work Sheet) for Statement of Cash Flows (continued)				
3					
4		Balance,	Transactions		Balance,
5	Account Title	______	Debit	Credit	______
6					
7					
8					
9					
10					
11					
12					
13					
14					
15					
16					
17					
18					
19					
20					
21					
22					
23					
24					
25					
26					
27					
28					
29					
30					
31					
32					
33					
34					
35					
36					
37					
38					
39					
40					
41					
42					
43					
44					
45					

PROBLEM 14-3 ___

Statement of Cash Flows

PROBLEM 14-3 ___, Continued

Statement of Cash Flows (continued)

PROBLEM 14-3 ___, Continued

The use of this form is not required unless so indicated by the instructor.

	A	B	C	D	E
1					
2	**Spreadsheet (Work Sheet) for Statement of Cash Flows**				
3					
4		**Balance,**	**Transactions**		**Balance,**
5	**Account Title**	________	**Debit**	**Credit**	________
6					
7					
8					
9					
10					
11					
12					
13					
14					
15					
16					
17					
18					
19					
20					
21					
22					
23					
24					
25					
26					
27					
28					
29					
30					
31					
32					
33					
34					
35					
36					
37					
38					
39					
40					
41					
42					
43					
44					
45					

PROBLEM 14-3 ___, Concluded

	A	B	C	D	E
1					
2	**Spreadsheet (Work Sheet) for Statement of Cash Flows (continued)**				
3					
4		**Balance,**	**Transactions**		**Balance,**
5	**Account Title**		**Debit**	**Credit**	
6					
7					
8					
9					
10					
11					
12					
13					
14					
15					
16					
17					
18					
19					
20					
21					
22					
23					
24					
25					
26					
27					
28					
29					
30					
31					
32					
33					
34					
35					
36					
37					
38					
39					
40					
41					
42					
43					
44					
45					

PROBLEM 14-4 ___

Statement of Cash Flows

PROBLEM 14-4 ___, Concluded

Computations:

PROBLEM 14-5 ___

Statement of Cash Flows

PROBLEM 14-5 ___, Concluded

Computations:

Name ______________________________

EXERCISE 15-1

a.

Comparative Income Statement

	Current Year Amount	Current Year Percent	Previous Year Amount	Previous Year Percent

b.

EXERCISE 15-2

a.

Comparative Income Statement (in thousands of dollars)

	CURRENT YEAR		PRIOR YEAR	
	AMOUNT	PERCENT	AMOUNT	PERCENT

EXERCISE 15-2, Concluded

b.

EXERCISE 15-3

a.

Common-Sized Income Statement

	TANNENHILL COMPANY		ELECTRONICS INDUSTRY AVERAGE
	AMOUNT	PERCENT	

b.

EXERCISE 15-4

Comparative Balance Sheet

	CURRENT YEAR		PREVIOUS YEAR	
	AMOUNT	PERCENT	AMOUNT	PERCENT

EXERCISE 15-5

a.

Comparative Income Statement

	CURRENT YEAR AMOUNT	PREVIOUS YEAR AMOUNT	INCREASE (DECREASE)	
			AMOUNT	PERCENT

EXERCISE 15-5, Concluded

b. ______________________

EXERCISE 15-6

a. (1) Working Capital = ______________________

Current Year: ______________________

Previous Year: ______________________

(2) Current Ratio = ______________________

Current Year: ______________________

Previous Year: ______________________

(3) Quick Ratio = ______________________

Current Year: ______________________

Previous Year: ______________________

b. ______________________

EXERCISE 15-7

a. (1) Current Ratio = ______________________

Current Year: ______________________

Prior Year: ______________________

(2) Quick Ratio = ______________________

Current Year: ______________________

Prior Year: ______________________

b. ______________________

EXERCISE 15-8

a. ______________________

b. ______________________

EXERCISE 15-9

a. (1) Accounts Receivable Turnover = ______________________

2016: ______________________

2015: ______________________

(2) Number of Days' Sales in Receivables = ______________________

2016: ______________________

2015: ______________________

b. ______________________

EXERCISE 15-10

a. (1) Accounts Receivable Turnover = ______________________

Xavier: ______________________

Lestrade: ______________________

(2) Number of Days' Sales in Receivables = ______________________

Xavier: ______________________

Lestrade: ______________________

EXERCISE 15-10, Concluded

b. ____________________

EXERCISE 15-11

a. (1) Inventory Turnover = ____________________

Current Year: ____________________

Preceding Year: ____________________

(2) Number of Days' Sales in Inventory = ____________________

Current Year: ____________________

Preceding Year: ____________________

b. ____________________

EXERCISE 15-12

a. (1) Inventory Turnover = ______________________

____

Dell: ______________________

____

HP: ______________________

____

(2) Number of Days' Sales in Inventory = ______________________

____

Dell: ______________________

____

HP: ______________________

____

b. ______________________

EXERCISE 15-13

a. Ratio of Liabilities to Stockholders' Equity = ______________________________

____

Current Year: ______________________________

____

Previous Year: ______________________________

____

b. Number of Times Bond Interest Charges Are Earned = ______________________________

____

Current Year: ______________________________

____

Previous Year: ______________________________

____

c. ______________________________

____

____

____

____

____

____

EXERCISE 15-14

a. Ratio of Liabilities to Stockholders' Equity = ______________________________

____

Hasbro: ______________________________

____

Mattel, Inc.: ______________________________

____

b. Number of Times Interest Charges Are Earned = ______________________________

____

Hasbro: ______________________________

____

Mattel, Inc.: ______________________________

____

EXERCISE 15-14, Concluded

c. ______________________

EXERCISE 15-15

a. Ratio of Liabilities to Stockholders' Equity = ______________________

Mondelez: ______________________

Hershey: ______________________

b. Ratio of Fixed Assets to Long-Term Liabilities = ______________________

Mondelez: ______________________

Hershey: ______________________

EXERCISE 15-15, Concluded

c. ______________________

EXERCISE 15-16

a. Ratio of Sales to Total Assets = ______________________

YRC Worldwide: ______________________

Union Pacific: ______________________

C.H. Robinson Worldwide Inc.: ______________________

EXERCISE 15-16, Concluded

b.

EXERCISE 15-17

a. Rate Earned on Total Assets = ____________________

2016: ____________________

2015: ____________________

Rate Earned on Stockholders' Equity = ____________________

2016: ____________________

2015: ____________________

Rate Earned on Common Stockholders' Equity = ____________________

2016: ____________________

2015: ____________________

b. ____________________

EXERCISE 15-18

a. Rate Earned on Total Assets = ____________________

Fiscal Year 3: ____________________

Fiscal Year 2: ____________________

b. Rate Earned on Stockholders' Equity = ____________________

Fiscal Year 3: ____________________

Fiscal Year 2: ____________________

c. ____________________

d. ____________________

EXERCISE 15-19

a. Ratio of Fixed Assets to Long-Term Liabilities = ______________________

b. Ratio of Liabilities to Stockholders' Equity = ______________________

c. Ratio of Sales to Assets = ______________________

d. Rate Earned on Total Assets = ______________________

e. Rate Earned on Stockholders' Equity = ______________________

f. Rate Earned on Common Stockholders' Equity = ______________________

EXERCISE 15-20

a. Number of Times Bond Interest Charges Are Earned = ______________________________

b. Number of Times Preferred Dividends Are Earned = ______________________________

c. Earnings per Share on Common Stock = ______________________________

d. Price-Earnings Ratio = ______________________________

e. Dividends per Share of Common Stock = ______________________________

f. Dividend Yield = ______________________________

EXERCISE 15-21

a. Earnings per Share = ______________________

b. Price-Earnings Ratio = ______________________

c. Dividends per Share = ______________________

d. Dividend Yield = ______________________

EXERCISE 15-22

a. Price-Earnings Ratio = ______________________

Deere & Co.: ______________________

Google: ______________________

The Coca-Cola Company: ______________________

Dividend Yield = ______________________

Deere & Co.: ______________________

Google: ______________________

The Coca-Cola Company: ______________________

b. ______________________

APPENDIX EXERCISE 15-23

a. Earnings per share on income before extraordinary items:

Earnings Before Extraordinary Items per Share on Common Stock = ______________________

b. Earnings per Share on Common Stock = ______________________

APPENDIX EXERCISE 15-24

a. ______________________

b. ______________________

c. ______________________

d. ______________________

e. ______________________

f. ______________________

g. ______________________

APPENDIX EXERCISE 15-25

a.

Partial Income Statement

b.

Partial Income Statement

APPENDIX EXERCISE 15-26

a. ______________________________

b. ______________________________

PROBLEM 15-1 ___

1.

Comparative Income Statement

	2016	2015	INCREASE (DECREASE)	
			AMOUNT	PERCENT

2.

This Page Not Used.

PROBLEM 15-2 ___

1.

Comparative Income Statement

	2016		2015	
	AMOUNT	PERCENT	AMOUNT	PERCENT

2.

This Page Not Used.

PROBLEM 15-3 ___

1. a. Working Capital = ______________________________

b. Current Ratio = ______________________________

c. Quick Ratio = ______________________________

PROBLEM 15-3 ___, Concluded

2.

Transaction	Working Capital	Current Ratio	Quick Ratio
a.			
b.			
c.			
d.			
e.			
f.			
g.			
h.			
i.			
j.			

Supporting Data:

Transaction	Current Assets	Quick Assets	Current Liabilities
a.			
b.			
c.			
d.			
e.			
f.			
g.			
h.			
i.			
j.			

PROBLEM 15-4 ___

1. through 19.

1. Working Capital: ____________________________

Ratio	Numerator	Denominator	Calculated Value
2. Current ratio			
3. Quick ratio			
4. Accounts receivable turnover			
5. Number of days' sales in receivables			
6. Inventory turnover			
7. Number of days' sales in inventory			
8. Ratio of fixed assets to long-term liabilities			
9. Ratio of liabilities to stockholders' equity			
10. Number of times interest charges are earned			
11. Number of times preferred dividends are earned			
12. Ratio of sales to assets			
13. Rate earned on total assets			
14. Rate earned on stockholders' equity			
15. Rate earned on common stockholders' equity			
16. Earnings per share on common stock			
17. Price-earnings ratio			
18. Dividends per share of common stock			
19. Dividend yield			

This Page Not Used.

PROBLEM 15-5 ___

1. a.

Rate Earned on Total Assets

Year

Rate Earned on Total Assets = ____________________

____

2016: ____________________

____

2015: ____________________

____

2014: ____________________

____

2013: ____________________

____

2012: ____________________

____

PROBLEM 15-5 ___, Continued

b.

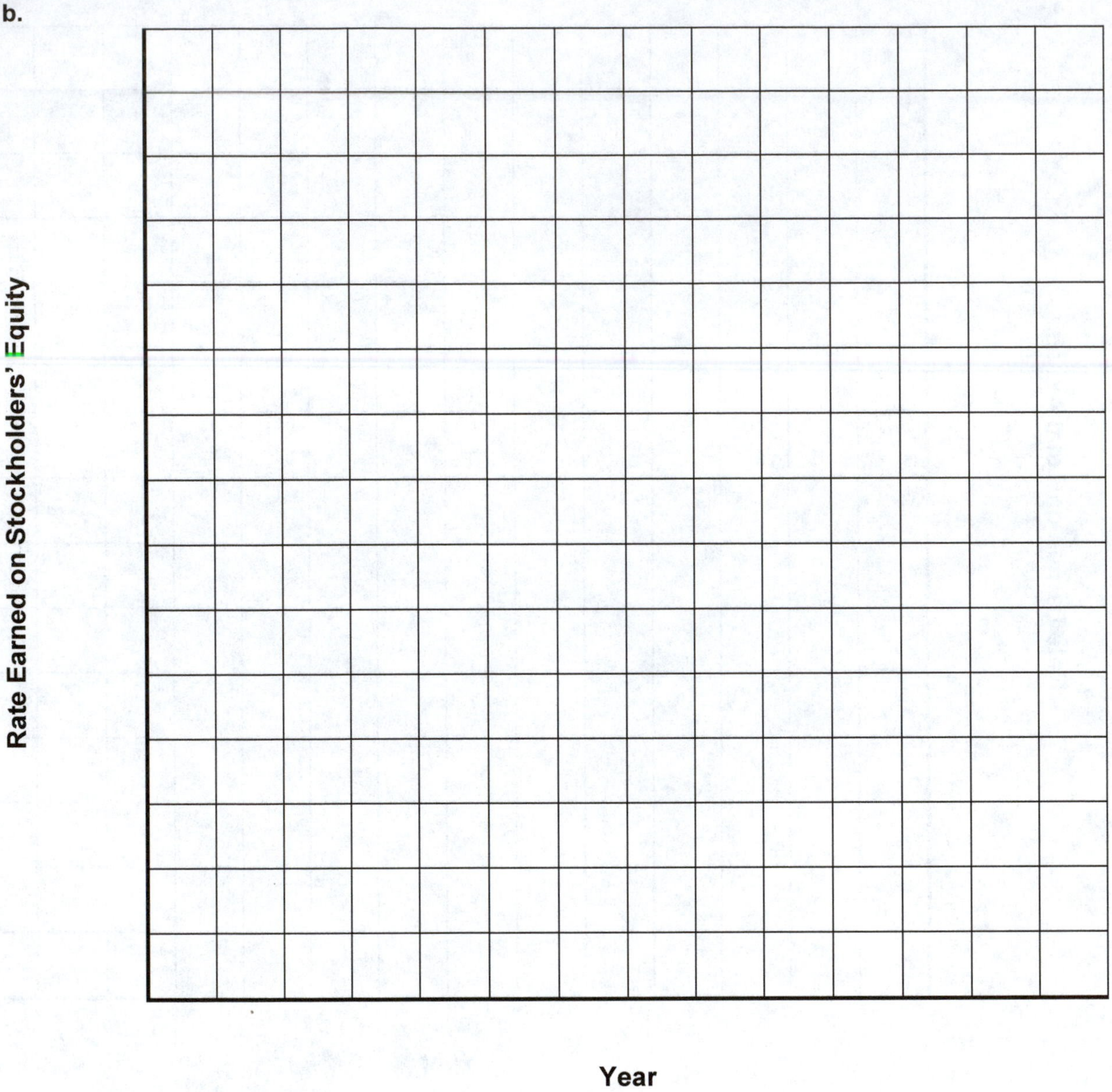

Rate Earned on Stockholders' Equity = ______________________________

____

2016: ______________________________

____

2015: ______________________________

____

2014: ______________________________

____

2013: ______________________________

____

2012: ______________________________

____

PROBLEM 15-5 ___, Continued

c.

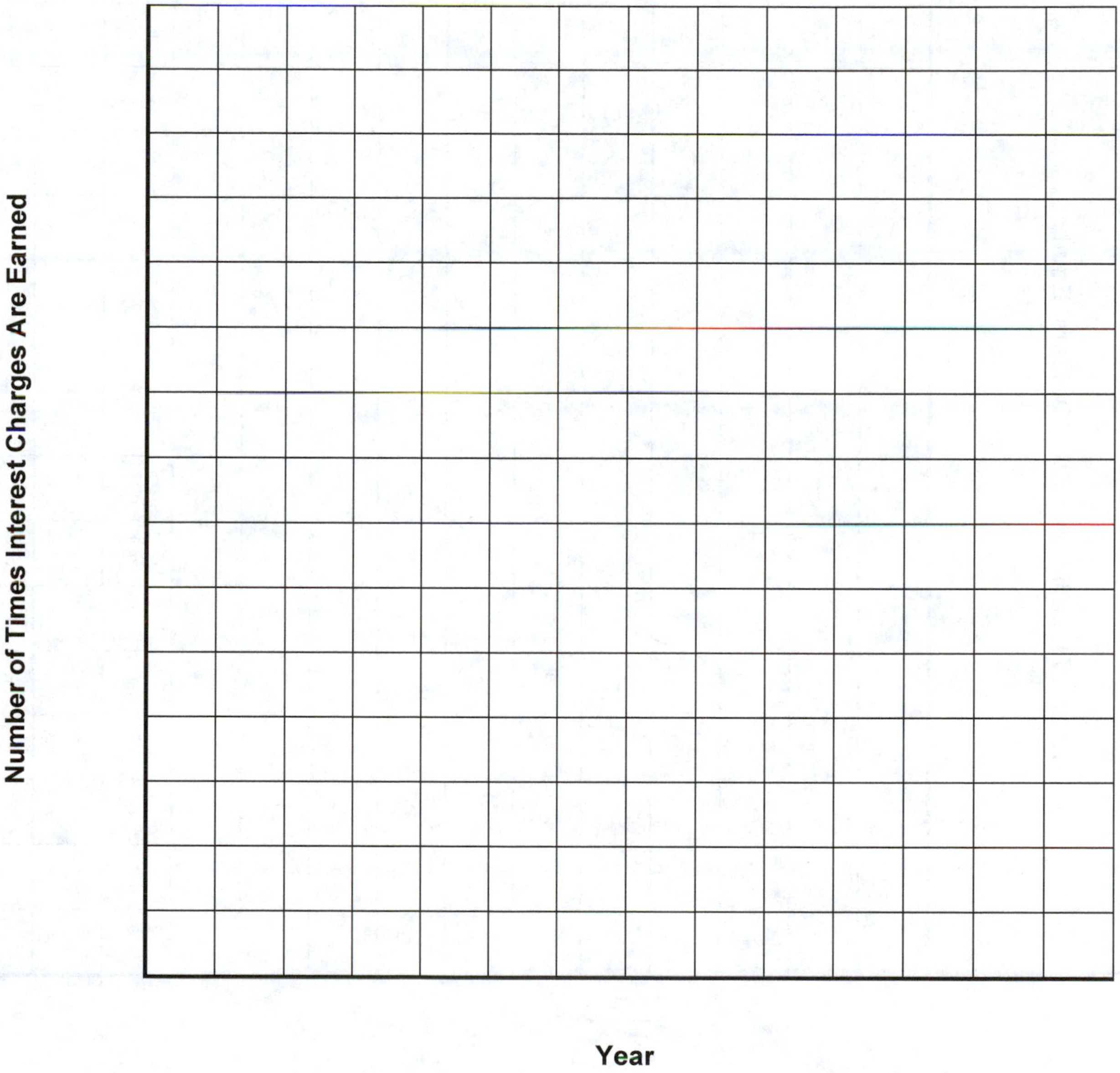

Number of Times Interest Charges Are Earned = ______________________________________

____

2016: ______________________________ 2013: ______________________________

______________________________ ______________________________

2015: ______________________________ 2012: ______________________________

______________________________ ______________________________

2014: ______________________________

____

PROBLEM 15-5 ___, Continued

d.

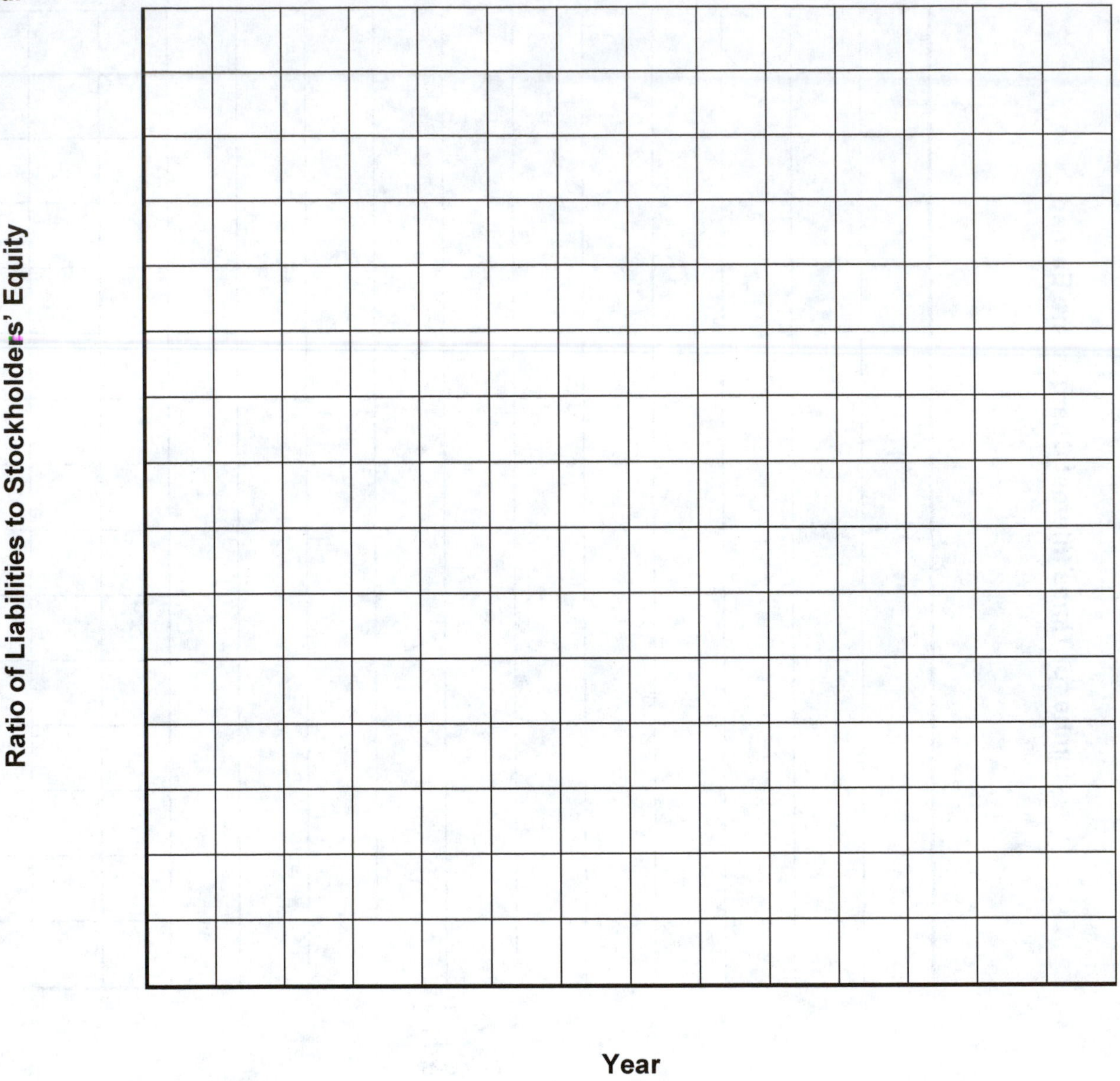

Ratio of Liabilities to Stockholders' Equity = ______________________________

____

2016: ______________________ 2013: ______________________

______________________ ______________________

2015: ______________________ 2012: ______________________

______________________ ______________________

2014: ______________________

____

PROBLEM 15-5 ___, Concluded

2.

This Page Not Used.

NIKE, INC., PROBLEM

1. a. through m.

	FISCAL 2012	FISCAL 2011

NIKE, INC., PROBLEM, Continued

	FISCAL 2012	FISCAL 2011

Name ______________________________

NIKE, INC., PROBLEM, Continued

	FISCAL 2012	FISCAL 2011

NIKE, INC., PROBLEM, Continued

2. a. through m.

NIKE, INC., PROBLEM, Concluded

This Page Not Used.

CPSIA information can be obtained
at www.ICGtesting.com
Printed in the USA
FFHW01n1030090718
47334951-50372FF

9 781285 869582